We Survived

THE

HOLOCAUST

We Survived

THE
HOLOCAUST

BY ELAINE LANDAU

FRANKLIN WATTS
NEW YORK/LONDON/TORONTO/SYDNEY

A NOTE ABOUT THE PHOTOGRAPHS

Many of these individuals survived the Holocaust with few, if any, belongings. Yet whenever possible, they have supplied a photograph from their youth for the book. The pictures do not necessarily coincide with the speaker's age during the Nazis' reign—some of the people may be older, while others are younger. However, these were the only photographs available, and we wanted you to see these people at another time, in what sometimes may seem like another world.

Photographs copyright ©: Leo Boech Institute, N.Y.C.: p. 17 (Eric Pollitzer); YIVO Institute for Jewish Research: pp. 79, 102; Joseph Sepkoski: all present-day photographs on pp. 14, 24, 30, 36, 42, 48, 58, 64, 74, 84, 90, 98, 106, 110, 120, 126; all other photographs are courtesy of the Holocaust survivors.

Library of Congress Cataloging-in-Publication Data

Landau, Elaine
We survived the Holocaust / Elaine Landau.
p. cm.
Includes bibliographical references and index.
Summary: A collection of the memoirs of sixteen Jewish Holocaust survivors.
ISBN 0–531–11115–6 (lib. bdg.)—ISBN 0–531–15229–4
1. Holocaust, Jewish (1939–1945)—Personal narratives—Juvenile literature. [1. Holocaust, Jewish (1939–1945)—Personal narratives. 2. Holocaust survivors. 3. Jews—Biography.]
I. Landau, Elaine.
D804.3.W39 1991
940.53′18′0922—dc20
[B]
91-16982 CIP AC

Contents

We Survived
THE
HOLOCAUST

Introduction

The true stories that unfold within this book occurred amid the turmoil of World War II, a conflict through which more lives were lost than in any previous war in history. Adolf Hitler, who became Germany's chancellor in January 1933, nurtured a national appetite for a more powerful, aggressive Germany. Anxious to annex new territory, in March 1938, Hitler absorbed Austria into Germany. Although an international agreement already afforded the German dictator a portion of Czechoslovakia, the following year he seized the remainder. Hitler furthered his dream of a German empire with his invasion of Poland on September 1, 1939. When Great Britain and France declared war on Germany the day Hitler's troops marched into Poland, World War II began.

In a militaristic flourish, German troops invaded and occupied Denmark, Luxembourg, Belgium, Norway, Holland, France, part of north Africa, and other areas. By 1940, Great Britain stood alone in its commitment to halt Hitler's aggression. Yet Hitler continued to delay an invasion of Britain, and instead sent his armies to conquer

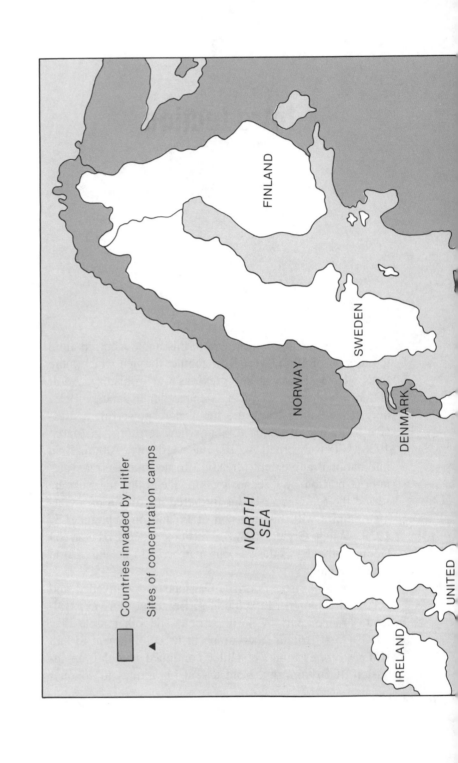

Countries invaded by Hitler

Sites of concentration camps

NORTH
SEA

IRELAND

UNITED

FINLAND

SWEDEN

NORWAY

DENMARK

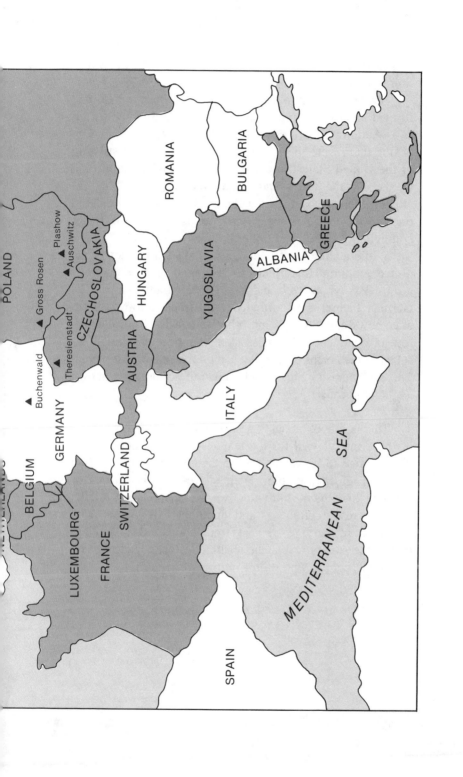

Yugoslavia and Greece. In June 1941, he used three million soldiers to invade Russia.

As the war continued, Germany and Italy, which had formed an alliance known as the Axis, were joined by Japan. Additional nations sided with the Axis as well. Opposing them were the Allies, a group of nations consisting of the United States, Great Britain, the Soviet Union, and China. By the war's end, many other nations had also aligned themselves with the Allies. Germany surrendered on May 7, 1945. A week prior to its fall, Adolf Hitler committed suicide by shooting himself.

While attempting to enlarge and sustain his newly acquired empire, Hitler had also engaged in a second war against less empowered and well defended adversaries. The German fuehrer masterminded a full-scale effort to obliterate Jews as well as some other minorities from the European continent. The mass slaughter he orchestrated resulted in the deaths of 6 million Jews and millions of others. This nightmarish extinction of human life came to be known as the Holocaust.

This is a book about Jewish Holocaust survivors. Many of those interviewed for the text were young people when Hitler's rise to power disrupted their lives in a way they never imagined possible. Their stories are the stories of millions like them. Individually, the accounts reflect the bravery, resourcefulness, and endurance of youths who struggled to survive against tremendous odds. Collectively, the stories reveal the shattered dreams and lives of the young people who didn't return.

1

Lewis Schloss—Germany

"I was born and raised in northwestern Germany in a region resembling the Pittsburgh area. My parents had a dry goods business which had been started by my grandfather. Now my grandfather, parents, and their three children (my two sisters and I) lived in an apartment above our store.

"I was just twelve years old when Hitler became chancellor. After only two months in power, the new German fuehrer authorized a boycott of Jewish businesses. We awoke one morning to find all of my father's store windows painted with Stars of David and such slogans as: 'Don't buy from Jews' and 'Boycott Jewish stores.' One of my earliest recollections of the period is that of being a young boy trying to scrape the paint from the glass.

"As the result of a worldwide protest, the boycott's intensity lessened, and there was a general feeling among Jews that Hitler's reign would be of short duration. There was no reason to believe that he'd remain in power longer than any of the previous regimes. Perhaps my father felt unrealistically secure since he'd already proved his loyalty to Germany by fighting valiantly for his country during

World War I. He'd even received the Iron Cross as well as another medal for battlefield bravery. He thought it inconceivable that anyone who knew him could ever regard him as a threat to Germany.

"During the next two years, we began to experience subtle changes in our surroundings. Children formerly involved with democratically oriented youth groups now became members of Hitler's Youth. Jewish children experienced occasional name-calling from them, but things didn't significantly deteriorate until the end of 1935.

"By then, the Nazi theory of superior and inferior races had been incorporated into both the law and the educational curriculum. Now the doctrine of Jewish inferiority was preached to us on a daily basis. It was then that I decided I didn't want to attend school anymore. I was only fifteen years old and had always planned on becoming an aeronautical engineer, but under the circumstances, such aspirations had become unrealistic. My parents and I agreed that I should learn a trade. If there wasn't a future for Jews in Germany and we had to emigrate, it would be advantageous to have a marketable skill. So I became an apprenticed wallpaper hanger and painter.

"In 1938 I applied for permission to enter the United States. I remember being very proud because my father had bought me a new navy blue blazer and a pair of gray pants to wear the day I went to the American consulate to fill out the necessary forms. I was put on a waiting list because so many others had applied before me. Although I didn't know it then, my number wouldn't be called for another three years.

"Meanwhile, anti-Semitic sentiment seemed to increase all around us. Many of our rights as German citizens had been taken away. However, perhaps the worst atrocities against Jews began on what has become known as Crystal Night, or the Night of Broken Glass. On November 9, 1938, we were awakened during the night by the sound of smashing glass. Hitler's Nazi followers had broken all the Jewish store windows.

"After they'd destroyed our store windows, they came upstairs to the apartment where we lived. The Nazis broke down our front door, destroyed our furniture, and threw our china out the windows. They pushed us around somewhat, but we were not seriously beaten, as we later heard other Jews were. When they left, we hoped it was over, but a few hours later a group of Hitler's storm troopers and Nazi police returned. They arrested both my father and me. My grandfather had been allowed to remain, as at that point they'd had orders to leave the old people alone.

"My father and I were in jail for about three weeks. It was only by sheer accident that we weren't shipped off to a concentration camp. We'd been scheduled for a transport to one, but the SS officer in charge of bringing prisoners to the railroad station had been late in meeting the connecting train. Therefore, the transport left without us and we were freed.

"We returned home to find our store still in terrible condition. The broken glass of Crystal Night remained scattered everywhere around the building. We were forced to sweep up the glass and pay a trucker to cart it away. Although the Jewish merchants affected had been insured for glass damage, the insurance companies were ordered to send all damage payments to the government. My father, along with the others in his position, had to use his own funds to replace the glass.

"Once what was left of the store was cleaned, my father was forced to sell the business to a Nazi party member for practically nothing. This process, which the Nazis called 'Aryanization,' was rapidly occurring throughout Germany. Everywhere, Jewish merchants were made to sell businesses that had been in their families for years for a mere fraction of what they should have received. But under Hitler's reign, Jews could no longer own and operate businesses.

During Kristallnacht, or the Night of Broken Glass,
November 9, 1938, synagogues in Germany were burned
by the Nazis.

"As a result, in spite of my youth, I became the major breadwinner for my family. I worked as a painter five days a week from eight o'clock in the morning until six at night, and half a day on Saturday, but was only paid twenty-five cents an hour for all my work. Our situation was worsened by the fact that my father was now only permitted to withdraw a small portion of his savings from the bank each month. We had barely enough to exist on.

"To protect my younger sisters from future harm, my parents put their two small daughters on trains to Holland. Following Crystal Night, both the Dutch and Belgian governments opened their doors to Jewish children without papers. This was a significant humanitarian gesture, as by then it was nearly impossible to secure visas. However, parents were not permitted to accompany them. My mother packed a small suitcase for each child and we prayed that they'd be safe.

"In the fall of 1940, we'd heard about a sudden expulsion of Jews from southern Germany. Although we didn't know where they'd been taken, we later learned that they were deported to Nazi concentration camps in southern France. We began to seriously fear for our safety. I felt somewhat relieved when in 1941 I was finally contacted by the American consulate. The official paperwork had been completed, and I was now eligible to enter America. But I soon learned that my good news came too late. By then Germany had invaded Russia and my planned escape route out of Germany was blocked. Previously, the way out for Jews had been to take the Trans-Siberian railroad to Manchuria. From there you'd travel on to Japan, Cuba, and, finally, the United States.

"As it was too late to get away, I tried to survive where I was. But before long we heard the disheartening news that numerous so-called resettlement camps for Jews were established in eastern Europe. Soon Jews began to be deported in droves. My family was among those who received notification papers for 'resettlement.' Although the Nazis did not inform us of our ultimate destination, we were put on a train heading east.

"We traveled for about six days, passing through a number of German towns. We rode on passenger trains rather than the cattle cars used later, so that German civilians would remain unaware of how we'd be treated. The Nazis didn't wish to evoke an outpouring of sympathy for the Jews. They counted on the more vocal and widespread anti-Semitic sentiments prevalent in other eastern European countries to allow them to act more brutally in different areas.

"Our trip through Germany went smoothly enough, but once we crossed the border into German-occupied Poland, the Nazis shut off the train's heat. The winter had been extremely cold that year, and, at times as we continued the trip, the temperature dropped to forty degrees below zero. People began to turn white from the cold.

"We finally arrived at the railroad station of Riga, Latvia. As we stepped down from the train, the SS was there to greet us with rifles and dogs. We were brought to the Riga ghetto, an area in which Jews were detained. Shortly after our arrival, the SS began killing many people. Some were hung for minor infractions of the rules. Others were selected to die because they were either very old, very young, or too ill to work.

"My parents and I were made to work strenuously through the worst weather conditions. Many people became frostbitten. In these instances, they usually died once gangrene set in. Conditions were further worsened by the dearth of food provided. During the day we'd usually only be given a bowl of hot water with an occasional cabbage leaf in it. If you were lucky, you might receive a small piece of bread.

"For the next two and a half years, my mother, father and I worked on a number of Nazi work details. Then in 1944 my father and I were shipped to the concentration

19

District Office Westphalia   Gelsenkirchen, the 13 November 1941
Reichsassociation of Jews   Klosterstr. 21
in Germany:
Bureau Gelsenkirchen   Mr./Mrs./Miss

....
Gelsenkirchen-

.... Str.

We are required by the Secret State Police (Gestapo)--State Police Office Gelsenkirchen--to inform you that you and your family members listed below have been selected for evacuation to the East.

With the utmost calm you will effect your emigration preparations within the next three weeks. The exact transport date will be announced later.

Each person may take along baggage up to 50 kg in a suitcase (not bulky goods) plus a sum of RM 50. This sum must be held readily available and the attached declaration must be completed and signed. Whoever cannot raise this amount should contact the bureau at once.

The enclosed property declarations must be completed by you--together with each and every family member--exact and truthful in every way. (By the head of household for each family.) In addition to the statements made on pages 5, 6 and 7, necessary proof, savings bank books, etc., must be enclosed.

The declarations must be turned in no later than
Tuesday, the 18 November 1941, 11 a.m.
at the office of the (Jewish) community.

This order is to be followed and obeyed under any and all circumstances.

Further instructions will follow.

District Office Westphalia
Reichsassociation of Jews in Germany:
Bureau Gelsenkirchen

(Hugo Israel Sternfeld)
Designate.

Family members: ....   Max Schloss

....   Julie Schloss

....   Ludwig Schloss

Translated from the original German
by Lewis R. Schloss

camp Buchenwald. There we heard about a satellite camp at a munitions factory work site where additional camp workers were needed. The factory was located in a German town only about eight miles from where we'd originally lived. Both my father and I volunteered to work there, and luckily we were accepted.

"In many ways the factory wasn't typical of the places where concentration camp inmates usually labored. It was surrounded by residential housing, and many of the foremen and supervisors were German civilians rather than SS guards. Once we arrived at the factory, my father and I trained as crane operators. However, after a few weeks there, our workday began to be interrupted by heavy Allied bombing raids. Destroying a munitions factory would seriously hinder Germany, so at night British bombers attacked, while during the day American pilots generally conducted the raids. Each time the air raid siren sounded, we had to run for shelter.

"After a heavy air raid, one of the civilian foremen became friendly with my father. He'd been impressed by the eloquence with which my father spoke German and was surprised to learn that we'd previously lived only miles from the factory. As it turned out, this foreman's brother was a good friend of my father's prior to the war. Through this man, we eventually made contact with a former Christian neighbor whom we'd also been quite close to. Our old neighbor occasionally provided us with extra food delivered by the friendly foreman. The neighbor also sent word that if we were able to escape, he'd provide a safe haven for us.

This is a translation of one of the documents the Schloss family received before being taken from their home by the Nazis. Note that they were even required to pay a sum of money while being forced to abandon their property.

"From then on, the foreman secretly began to smuggle in civilian clothes for us. We hid the garments within a compartment of the crane we operated. I had some artistic ability and with various materials provided us by the foreman, I worked on forging passes for my father and myself. We'd hoped to escape during one of the frequent air raids, but, unfortunately, the guards were usually tripled during these periods, as the SS reasoned that would be the most opportune escape time.

"Yet one day I noticed only one guard on gate duty. Although I couldn't account for the lack of staff, I knew this was the day we had to make our move. During the lunch break, I found my father, and together we climbed into the cab of our crane where we couldn't be seen changing into our civilian clothes. To further disguise our appearance, we both wore caps. I put on the glasses people had been used to seeing my father wear. I could hardly see with them while he could hardly see without them, but we managed to safely climb down the fifty-foot crane ladder.

"Then we had to walk through a hall the size of a football field, past both fellow prisoners and SS officers. None of them recognized us, as it was inconceivable for them to even think of a prisoner not wearing prison stripes. It was broad daylight, but we just kept walking through the hall, along the outside fence, and past the gate to freedom.

"We walked to our former neighbor's house about six miles away, arriving at dusk. When we knocked on his door, our neighbor answered it. We said hello and he said hello in return. But after about three hellos, we realized that he still hadn't recognized us. Finally, my father asked, 'Don't you know who I am?' His friend admitted that he didn't. We'd grown quite thin and pale due to the scant rations we'd received. It was a frightening moment, but when my father identified himself, the man embraced us and took us into his home. We remained at his house as

22

well as that of his brother until April 10, 1945, when we were liberated by the American army."

Author's note: Mr. Schloss eventually married a young Jewish girl named Trudy whom he met while at a camp. Trudy had narrowly escaped being killed by the SS. Near the end of the war she, along with a number of other Jewish inmates, was locked in a farmer's barn by a group of SS guards. She suspected that the guards intended to set fire to the barn so that those inside would be burned alive. This way, the guards would immediately rid themselves of remaining prisoners who could later act as witnesses against them.

Too exhausted and starved to offer any resistance, the prisoners sat awaiting their fate, when they heard gunfire coming from outside the barn. Russian tanks passing through had seen the SS uniforms and shot the guards without even knowing about the prisoners locked in the barn. The inmates managed to free themselves, and Trudy was later able to reunite with Lewis. The couple now live in America, where they recently celebrated the birth of their first grandchild.

2
Esther Clifford—Germany

"In 1921 I arrived in Frankfurt, Germany, as an infant in my mother's arms. I was the youngest of her five children, and our parents had just moved our whole family to this city from the German town of Munich. A few years earlier, my parents emigrated to Germany from Poland and had tried living in various German cities while searching for a place they could call home.

"My mother and father did their best to create a close, loving family environment for us. However, any illusions we had of living a normal life faded as Hitler came to power. The impact of Nazism on our lives began subtly enough. First, my parents' Christian friends started to avoid them, and I noticed that each time I played with one of my Christian friends, her mother always called her to come home. My father owned a small leather goods shop, and now some of our former customers hesitated to patronize our establishment.

"But perhaps one of my most unsettling childhood memories occurred on a day I'd gone shopping with my mother. We noticed a group of people standing around a huge bonfire. We were shocked as we watched both storm troopers and local residents burning books by Jewish authors. We couldn't believe that this was happening in Germany, a country known for its advanced culture and outstanding achievements in music, art, and science. Incredibly, Hitler and the Nazi party appeared to be thriving.

"I was fortunate in attending an outstanding German-Jewish school. Yet by 1935, it became a challenge for a Jewish child to attend any school in Germany. We had to be creative in finding new routes to school each day. Usually groups of Christian public school students stood ready to pelt us with rocks and an assortment of other projectiles if they spotted us on the street. At times, Hitler Youths evaded school entirely, and simply spent most of their day attacking Jewish students. The situation grew so dangerous that my parents had to take us out of school.

"Our family suffered economically as well. One evening my father returned home looking extremely agitated. The Nazis had refused to renew his business license. They told him that all Jews who'd moved to Germany from Poland, as my father had, would be subject to this new restriction. My father had to close the store and secretly fashion handbags and various other leather items working within the confines of a large closet. I recall how as children we'd take turns standing guard at the window to warn him if a Nazi approached. After dark, my father would hide the merchandise under a large coat as he delivered it to the homes of former customers he trusted.

"By 1937, it looked as though Hitler wasn't going to disappear, so instead we decided to leave the country. Yet it wasn't easy to find a place to go. Everywhere we looked, quotas or restrictions of one type or another hampered our efforts. We followed every lead and listened to every story. We heard of families who'd fled to Cuba, Argentina, or China. But it soon became obvious that the world wasn't welcoming German Jews with open arms.

"As we waited to leave, I learned to make hats and

my sister became a skilled dressmaker. We hoped that
having a useful skill would enhance our chances of gaining
entry into a safe country. Having been impoverished by
the Nazis hadn't made us very desirable, but sometimes it
felt as if the world had conspired to keep us in Germany.

"Then on October 28, 1938, five uniformed Nazis came
to our home, broke down the door, and stormed into our
apartment. They told us that we were being deported to
Poland and had only five minutes to gather our things. The
Nazis herded us out of our apartment and into an open
truck outside in which a group of people already stood.
The soldiers continued making stops to pick up other Jews
until the truck was filled.

"We were taken to a Frankfurt prison and shoved into
a cell. As the hours passed, more families joined us. Finally, it felt as though we scarcely had room to breathe.
That night we were taken by truck from the prison to the
railway station. Within moments we were on a train bound
for Poland. You can't imagine the hopelessness and despair we felt, crammed into a train without food or water.
We weren't given anything to eat that day in prison and
some people had already fainted from hunger.

"Once we passed the last German town, between fifteen hundred and two thousand of us were ordered from
the train and made to walk to the Polish border. We marched
five abreast while the Nazis accompanied us with their rifles pointed at our backs.

"As we passed the last German checkpoint, we were
ordered to present our ID cards to the guards, while keep-
ing our hands held high in the air. Being under eighteen,
I didn't have an ID card yet, but was instead listed on my
father's. Since I had nothing to present, I hadn't held my
hands up. A German storm trooper noticed that and ordered me from the line. My parents tried to explain that I
was underage, but he wouldn't listen.

"After presenting their passes, my family had tightly
held hands so as not to be separated. However, when the

storm trooper raised his rifle butt to unclasp our human chain, I purposefully broke away so that no one would be hurt. I was ordered to face a wall several feet away. Next to me stood a woman with a child in one hand and a diaper in the other. There were also about one hundred others who'd been ordered from the line for one reason or another. I remember hoping that my family wouldn't have to watch if I were shot.

"As I turned my head slightly, I was relieved to see my family, along with the other marchers, proceeding past the border. At least my parents wouldn't have to see their youngest child killed. Meanwhile, as I waited there, I tried to think of the quickest, least painful way to die.

"However, I wasn't killed. Instead, we were put on trucks and driven to another German town. As the truck passed the remaining marchers, I looked for my family but couldn't find them. I never saw my mother, father, sister, or brother again.

"We were taken to a synagogue which the Nazis had converted to a prison. During the day, the Nazis permitted us to walk in the yard. Since they hadn't facilities to feed us, the guards allowed the town's German Jews to bring us food, which they'd push beneath the fence. In the days that followed, special bonds developed between us and the local Jews. Younger people tended to bring food for people their own age, while older people brought dishes for those who were more mature.

"Then one day a teenager who'd fed us confided that the gate was open and that the guard had momentarily left his post. Four or five of us quickly slipped out and were taken by car to the railway station. Those kind people put me on a train to my hometown of Frankfurt. I don't know what happened to the other escapees.

"I returned to our old Frankfurt apartment building, where a Christian neighbor took pity on me. As he'd had a key to our apartment, he let me in and told me not to make any noise. I gave him a pair of candlesticks in return for some money. Then, out of sheer exhaustion, I fell into a deep, comalike sleep.

"When I awoke, I knew it was too dangerous to remain at the apartment. I was able to stay with friends for a time, then with a former teacher, and finally with still another friend. Many times I had to leave quickly through a back door as the Nazis approached.

"In August 1939, I was living with a close girlfriend and her family. By then I'd been in hiding for about nine months. My girlfriend had a visa to England that had been issued to some Jewish teenagers willing to work there as maids. For a Jew in Nazi Germany, a visa to England was equivalent to a winning lottery ticket.

"However, the girl's parents did not want their daughter to go on without them, and felt that a family visa would soon be forthcoming. They gave her visa to me in anticipation that once I arrived in England, I might be able to speed the issuance of their group visa. When I later made the proper inquiries in England, I was informed that their visa was in fact going out any day. But just then the war broke out and my girlfriend and her family never escaped.

"In the years that followed, I learned that my deported family members had been taken to the Warsaw ghetto and probably perished in an extermination camp. Only two of my older married sisters who'd no longer lived with us at the time of the deportation survived. One managed to flee to China, the other to France. Of course, had it not been for some courageous people who'd helped me along the way, I probably would not have survived. Yet it's chilling to think that my survival initially stemmed from the actions of a heartless German storm trooper who pulled a young Jewish girl away from her parents as they clung together in a deportation line."

3

Henry Frank—Germany

"There were five children in my family—I had four sisters, and I was the only boy. We lived in Berlin, Germany, where I'd been born. Since we resided in Germany and my father fought in the German army during World War I, we tended to think of ourselves not as German Jews but as Germans. We'd assumed the German mentality, and we were proud, patriotic, and steeped in German tradition.

"Our family was quite poor. War injuries left my father an invalid and, as a result, his earning capacity was diminished. I grew up in a poor mixed neighborhood of both Christians and Jews. While many of my childhood friends were Christian, I don't recall ever having heard them express anti-Jewish sentiments. I first experienced this type of thinking in 1933 after Hitler came to power and a surge of anti-Semitism swept through local neighborhoods. Initially, my friends didn't abandon me. They viewed me as the one exception to what they were now told about Jews. Often they'd say things like, 'You're a good Jew, you're not like the others.'

"It was hard to adjust to what was happening, as all

31

of a sudden we were no longer considered German. What was once our religion, just as other Germans might be Protestant or Catholic, became both our sole nationality and identity. I had to face the fact that we were now disliked, and in time wouldn't even be tolerated in our own country. An anti-Jewish newspaper was published and distributed throughout the area. They printed crude caricatures of Jews with long beards and large hooked noses. The boldly typed headlines read, THE JEWS ARE OUR DOWNFALL.

"Slowly, restrictions were placed on the activities of Jews. Signs that read NO JEWS were placed on park benches. I couldn't play in the parks or go to the movies. Soon a curfew was imposed on us and we weren't allowed outside after seven in the evening. Aryans were also not to date or associate socially with non-Aryans. We didn't like what was happening around us, but hoped it wouldn't last.

"Although by 1935–36 my family no longer felt comfortable in Germany, we had few choices. Many affluent Jews were able to buy their way out of Germany and purchase citizenship in other countries. But if you were poor, the door slammed tightly shut on you.

"By then, Jews could be beaten, abused, or arrested. A Jewish friend and I were arrested at the 1936 Olympics just for laughing and having a good time. Although I was released soon after, it was a frightening experience. I was also required to check in daily with the local police for a month.

"Individuals involved in interfaith dating were now publicly humiliated and punished. One Christian girl caught secretly dating a Jewish boy had to wear a large sign which read, I'M THE BIGGEST PIG IN TOWN BECAUSE I DATED A JEWISH BOY.

"By 1938 every Jew was required to wear a yellow Star of David on his clothing and carry a special identification card with a large J on it for Jew. In Germany, all

Jews had a special middle name printed on their ID cards to make doubly certain their identity was not mistaken. The men were all given the middle name. of Israel, while the women had to take Sara as their new middle name. Our identification cards had our photographs and fingerprints as well.

"As a young man, the Nazis forced me, along with a number of other young Jews, to work on a construction crew. We worked from six in the morning until five in the afternoon. Even prior to the war's outbreak, we'd already seen troubling signs. Some Jews were said to have been put on transports and never heard from again.

"Once the war began in September 1939, the Nazis took me from the construction crew to work in a war supplies factory. Although Jews were still permitted to live at home, now we had to hang a large sign on our apartment doors which read JUDE [JEW]. As food became scarce, Jews were especially affected by the shortages. Since there was a J printed on our ration cards, we only received about a quarter of the rations allotted to Christians.

"We existed under austere conditions, but the full extent of Nazi brutality didn't personally touch our family until Nazi leader General Reinhardt Heydrich was assassinated. Heydrich was killed in Prague, Czechoslovakia, by non-Jewish partisans working with the underground against the Nazis. Although we had nothing to do with his death, the Gestapo immediately rounded up fifty Jewish men in Berlin, Germany. The men were lined up in front of a brick wall and shot to death. My father was one of them.

"The very next day my mother, sister, and I were picked up by the Gestapo and deported to a camp in Czechoslovakia known as Theresienstadt. While I was there, the living conditions weren't nearly as bad as in other concentration camps. At least we were given some food to eat. The Nazis designed Theresienstadt as a model camp to trick the outside world into believing that Jews hadn't been mistreated by Hitler. When the International Red Cross came to inspect camp conditions for themselves, the Nazis printed up and distributed money to us to foster an illusion of prosperity. But a close examination of the bills would have revealed that the currency wasn't genuine and afforded us no further purchasing power.

"After a while I, along with a number of others, was taken from Theresienstadt to a site near Berlin where we worked on a construction crew building lodgings for Gestapo officers. I remained on the project for about a year. We did hard physical labor daily for at least fifteen-hour shifts. At night we slept on a wooden board. At times the guards' treatment of us was extremely harsh. Once when a guard felt I wasn't working fast enough, he hit me in the mouth with a large steel pipe, knocking out all my teeth. I also acquired a number of scars from the frequent beatings. Yet regardless of the circumstances, I was glad to be there because we were promised that our relatives at Theresienstadt would not be sent to cruder camps in eastern Europe, where many Jews perished. As my mother, sisters, and small nieces were still at Theresienstadt, I counted on my hard work to save their lives.

"But in 1944, as the Russian army advanced toward our work site, the construction effort was halted and we were taken back to Theresienstadt by cattle car. When I arrived, I learned that they lied about our relatives' assured safety to make us work harder and discourage escape attempts. My mother, sisters, and young nieces were not at Theresienstadt to welcome me back. I could only assume they'd died elsewhere in Nazi gas chambers.

"I was only back at Theresienstadt about a month when I became one of forty young men selected to go to Bavaria [an area in south Germany]. Once again I did construction work to build housing for Gestapo personnel. But we didn't stay there very long as the war was nearly over and Allied forces were rapidly taking territory all around us. The SS interrupted our work and we began the long march back to Theresienstadt. The trip took seven days and nights on foot.

We were also required to pull heavy wagons as we traveled.

"When we finally arrived at Theresienstadt, a woman ran up to me, threw her arms around me, and said, 'Oh Henry, it's so wonderful to see you.' I looked at her in astonishment and wondered who she was. Then she said, 'Don't you know me, Henry? It's Inge.' I hadn't recognized the bald, emaciated girl who stood before me, but it was my own sister—the only member of my family who survived the Holocaust with me. Before long, the International Red Cross arrived at the camp, and shortly thereafter we were liberated by the Russian army. Now it was the German guards and SS who ran for their lives rather than the Jews.

"Eventually, I came to America, where I prospered. Once a supervisor at my place of employment noticed the speed and precision of my work and jokingly told me, 'Slow down, Henry, you're not in a concentration camp any longer.'

"Today, when my wife and I lecture in public schools on the Holocaust, we stress the inherent danger in the myth of racial superiority. As we tell the students, 'According to the Old Testament, first God created Heaven and Earth. Then he created Adam and Eve. But the Bible doesn't specify whether Adam and Eve were black, white, Asian, or Hispanic. God simply created two human beings. To coexist, we must respect one another. Everyone born on this Earth has a right to live. There are no second-rate human beings, and none of us can afford to think that there are.' "

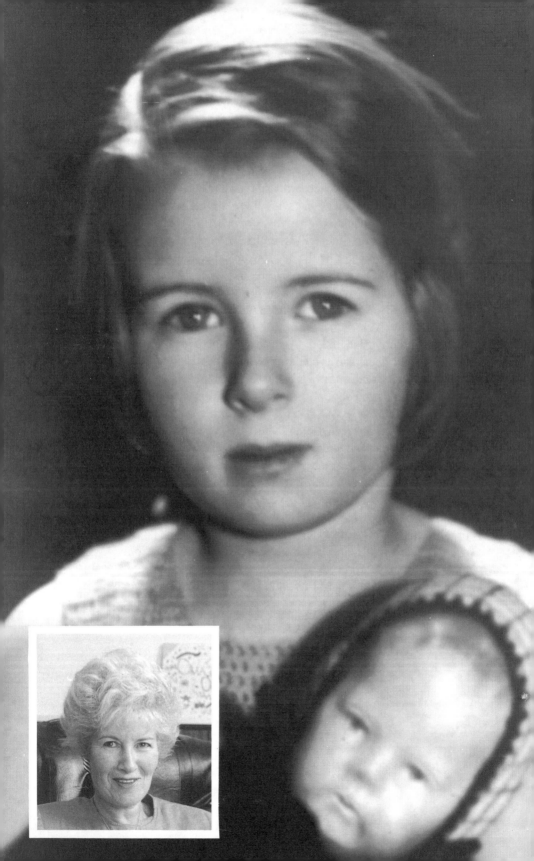

4
Irene Frank—Germany

"I was born in Berlin, Germany, in 1927, the only child of an extremely wealthy Jewish family. My father had inherited a large, successful moving and shipping business from my grandfather, and I'd enjoyed a prosperous childhood. Due to the nature of my father's business, he was instrumental in helping many Jewish families flee from Germany as Hitler became powerful. But by the time we realized that we'd better leave ourselves, our path was blocked.

"Prior to Hitler, my family hadn't felt the sting of religious prejudice. We had a fairly large number of Christian friends and were well integrated within our neighborhood's social fabric. But when I began school, trouble was already on the horizon, and by 1938 I was no longer able to attend classes. Jews were also required to wear yellow stars, which at times led to some amusing incidents for one of my girlfriends and me. As we were both blond and blue eyed, we looked so typically Aryan that most people thought we were Christian. More than once when walking together down a busy city street, Gentile adults would stop us and

37

say, 'Girls, take off those stars. You don't have to wear them. Only Jews are required to wear that symbol.'

"Between 1939 and 1940, the Nazis took my father's business. After losing everything, he was made to do forced labor for them. Meanwhile, Jews were being put on trains and deported to concentration camps in Poland. We were selected for deportation as well, but were saved merely by circumstance. My father's work supervisor felt that my father was too productive a worker to lose. So he managed to have our family's name removed from the list of those scheduled to leave.

"The Nazis also forced my mother to work in an electronics factory. Something hideous must have happened to her there. She was crying when she returned from her first day of work. She looked at me and said that she was tired and needed to rest. She went into her bedroom to lie down and said that she didn't want to be disturbed. When my father came home later, he was unable to wake her. It was then that we realized she'd taken an overdose of sleeping pills and committed suicide. I was fourteen years old at the time.

"Following my mother's death in 1941, my grandmother moved in to take care of me and cook for us. While we remained in Berlin, the Allies bombed the city nearly every day. After a while, I no longer bothered to undress for bed. I knew that every few hours we had to go down to the basement for protection in case our building was hit.

"My grandmother was only with us for about a year before the Nazis deported her to the Theresienstadt concentration camp in Czechoslovakia. About two months later, we received a letter that my father and I were to be picked up and deported the following morning. True to their word, early the next day, SS men came for us. We were only permitted to bring a bedroll and a few possessions. They sealed off our apartment and put us on one of the trucks waiting outside.

"After being detained in a central holding area for a

few days, we were brought to the train station. But while we waited on the platform to board the train, I noticed that the guards had ransacked our bedrolls and suitcases. They were searching for valuables their Jewish prisoners might have secretly taken along. Once we were seated on the train, the SS announced in each car, 'We've checked your belongings. If you have jewelry, money, or any other item of worth on your person, place it in the large hat we are passing around. This is your last opportunity to give us whatever you have. If you don't, and it's found on you, you'll be immediately shot.' I knew my father had taken both money and diamonds along, so I begged him to go to the rest room and flush it all down the toilet. He did so, because even throwing our money away was preferable to giving it to the Nazis.

"Our train ride ended at Theresienstadt. After only being there a week, I came down with scarlet fever. I was quarantined for six weeks, but no medication was available. After I began to recover, I did farm work in the fields with a group of other young people. We'd get up early in the morning and stand on line for roll call. On one occasion, the entire camp was made to stand for forty-eight hours for roll call. We weren't permitted to eat or sleep during those days. It was quite cold at the time, and not everyone could obey. Some collapsed from exhaustion, others even died.

"As time passed, the transports out of Theresienstadt to the East were more frequent. But we were only told that we were going to another labor camp. In September 1944, my father, along with many others, was put into a crowded cattle car and deported. I never saw him after that. Two months later, I was taken from the camp on a transport as well. As hundreds of us were shoved into cattle cars, we felt like matchsticks packed into a matchbox. Since there were no rest room facilities, people were forced to urinate on one another during the long train ride. Then the train finally stopped at the Auschwitz concentration camp.

"When we arrived, they shaved our heads and made

us take off our clothes. I was only given a thin shirt to wear and the weather had already begun to turn cold. The barracks we slept in had a roof, but no walls or doors. Since it was like an open-air horse stable, we were especially cold at night.

"Everywhere you looked there was dirt and mud. You'd often find yourself forced to walk through mud up to your knees. Each day you were marched through the slush to the latrine. While inmates defecated, guards with whips stood behind them to ensure that these bodily functions were speedily performed.

"I remember seeing a young teenage girl break down before my eyes. One day after roll call, she got up off the board we slept on, walked to the center of the barracks, and started singing. Then she went outside and hurled her body against the electrified camp fence. She was instantly electrocuted.

"But despite our predicament, many of us still had hope. Of course, at the time, we didn't know about the gas chambers. We saw smoke from the crematoriums, but were led to believe that it came from a factory operating in that part of the camp.

"I was at Auschwitz for four weeks before the Nazis placed me on a transport headed for still another camp. After arriving, I was put to work in a factory weaving cloth on a flax machine. Sometimes I think that job saved my life, because I was able to eat the tiny seeds I found inside the flax. As I worked, I could also wrap the flax around my knees for warmth. Nevertheless, our workload was punishing. I wove for sixteen hours a day and then spent several hours unloading the train cars of coal arriving daily to fuel the cloth factory.

"There were four hundred young women at the camp and we were given nearly nothing to eat. We were starving and desperate. One day a horse dropped dead in the yard behind our factory building. We were so famished that we cut ourselves pieces of the animal, which we ate raw.

"I remained at that camp until the Russians liberated us in May. Prior to the Russians' arrival, the SS tried to march us to another area, but they decided the Russians were too near, so instead we were marched back to our former camp. The SS officers locked us in the various factory buildings and then, hoping to evade capture, fled in different directions. Two days later, the Russians arrived and freed us. But a number of Russian soldiers failed to act heroically. Unfortunately, many of the women inmates were raped by the men who supposedly came to help them.

"I later came to the United States. When I arrived in America, I only had five dollars in my pocket. But I immediately went to work and was able to find an inexpensive furnished room in New York City. I remained close to many of the young Holocaust survivors who also left Europe. Henry Frank, the man I eventually married, was among them. We've been married for forty-two years and have two children and five grandchildren. Hitler's dream didn't come true. We survived the Holocaust. We were born as Jews and we will live and die as Jews in America."

5

Ralph Katz—Germany

"During the late 1930s, it became increasingly difficult for Jews in Germany. My parents sent my older brother to a highly respected Jewish school in Frankfurt, known as the Philanthropin. While he attended public school, he'd been beaten up nearly every day in the schoolyard because he was a Jew. In any case, before long, Jewish children weren't even permitted to attend public school.

"My parents also tried to shield me from the Nazis. In 1938, when I was just six years old, they sent me to a summer camp in Switzerland so I'd be out of Germany for a while. It was unusual for such a young child to travel alone internationally, but those were unusual times.

"After Crystal Night, when many Jewish businesses and synagogues were burned and destroyed, the Gestapo came looking for my father. They were arresting Jewish men over sixteen years of age, so my brother and I were too young to be taken yet. But the Gestapo officers couldn't find my father, as only a week before our family had moved in order to hide from them. Fortunately, we didn't have to remain in hiding very long, since following Crystal Night there was somewhat of an international outcry over what transpired. Many of the men arrested that night or shortly thereafter and sent to concentration camps were released. And, at least for a while, the Nazis ceased deporting German Jews.

"This may sound strange, but in a way Crystal Night was like a godsend because it warned us of things to come. Many German-Jewish families began to plan their departures. My father was among those who'd grown concerned, but it was difficult to find a place to go. America, along with numerous other countries, was in an economic depression, and somewhat reluctant to welcome large numbers of refugees to add to those already seeking work.

"By the 1920s, the U.S. had already cut down on the number of immigrants allowed into the country. In order to come, you needed a sponsor. My father wrote to some distant American relatives he'd never met to ask them to sponsor us. However, a sponsor had to post a twenty-five-dollar bond, and our relatives said they couldn't afford to help us. But my father continued to write to them, describing the urgency of the situation, while pleading for assistance. Eventually, they posted the bond.

"In early 1939, my father was the first of us to leave. Once he found work in the States he tried to bring us over. During this period, German Jews scattered to wherever they could find asylum. Sadly, some went to Poland, Russia, and eastern France, where they later encountered the Nazis for a second time. Others fled to distant countries in South America and survived.

"Meanwhile, Hugo Steinhardt, the headmaster of my brother's Frankfurt school, feared for the safety of his Jewish students, who were thought to be among the brightest and the best in Germany. Believing the boys' lives were in danger, Steinhardt wrote to affluent, prominent Jews throughout the world asking them to secure refuge for the students in their countries.

"Finally a reply came through a representative of James

and Dorothy de Rothschild of the English branch of the international banking family. They agreed to rescue any boy at the school from Nazi Germany whose parents would allow him to come to England. The boys ranged in age from eight to fifteen. Some of the parents found it too difficult to part with their children, and many who remained later died.

"My brother was among the boys who went. The students traveled part of the way to England by railway and were passengers on what became known as the Kinder Transport, or Children's Train. Actually, the Kinder Transport, which was filled with Jewish boys and girls, was part of a larger effort to rescue endangered children from the Nazis' domain. The schoolboys took the train to Holland, where they boarded a boat for England.

"After arriving in England in March 1939, they settled in a large Victorian house, which had once been used as a hospital. The dwelling, secured for the students by the Rothschilds, was located near the Rothschild mansion. As there were three huge cedar trees planted on the property, the students became known as the Cedar Boys.

"Although I'd been too young to attend the school, I received permission to join my brother and the others in England. The only way my mother could get me out of Germany was to put me on a train to Hamburg wearing a large identification tag, so I'd be recognized by our contact person. That individual met me at the train stop, and from there brought me to a ship bound for England. Three days later, I arrived in a new country to join the refugee students. I was seven years old at the time and had already reluctantly taken two international trips to avoid Nazi persecution.

"My brother and I remained in England for about a year while attending public school. Although some of the boys had never been out of Germany before, we learned English because the headmaster forced us to speak it. The Cedar Boys escaped the Nazi gas chambers, but even under the best of circumstances, it was a difficult time. We were far from home and worried about our families. Some of the boys were so affected by the trauma and confusion that bed-wetting was not uncommon. Two of the older boys were even detained by the British in another area. Although they were Jewish teenagers, the British thought they might be Hitler Youth spies or saboteurs posing as Jewish refugees to gain sympathy.

"In August 1939, my father brought my mother to America. Then in May 1940, my brother and I arrived in the United States. We just missed Germany's heavy bombing of England by a few days. As we moved from country to country, sometimes it felt as though we were dodging bullets. Even while aboard an English vessel to America, our captain tried to avoid German submarines, as naval warfare was already a frightening aspect of civilian travel.

"My family settled in New York, where I tried to become the all-American boy. I was determined to put the Holocaust behind me, refusing to allow the feelings and memories associated with it to surface for nearly thirty years. Although as an adult, I taught European history in public school, I never told my students that I was there when what I taught them occurred. Then in 1970, on a European vacation, I revisited both Germany and my past. I returned to Europe several times since, but genuinely relived my experiences as a Cedar Boy in England several years later through an ironic chance encounter.

"My brother, who was also a Cedar Boy, became an engineer. While working on a special project in New York City, he consulted with another engineer associated with the job. Once the two men saw one another, each acknowledged that the other looked familiar. Trying to discern if they'd previously met, they stumbled on the remarkable coincidence that both had been Cedar Boys. After that chance meeting, the three of us actively tried to locate other Cedar Boys and planned a reunion at the English house where we'd stayed as children.

"While all the Cedar Boys lost relatives during the Holocaust, some were the sole survivors of their families. Many of these boys became extremely prominent adults. Among them are professors from Yale University and the London School of Economics, two physicians, and numerous successful businessmen and professionals. They were rescued boys given the opportunity to grow into fine men. Child survivors of the Holocaust."

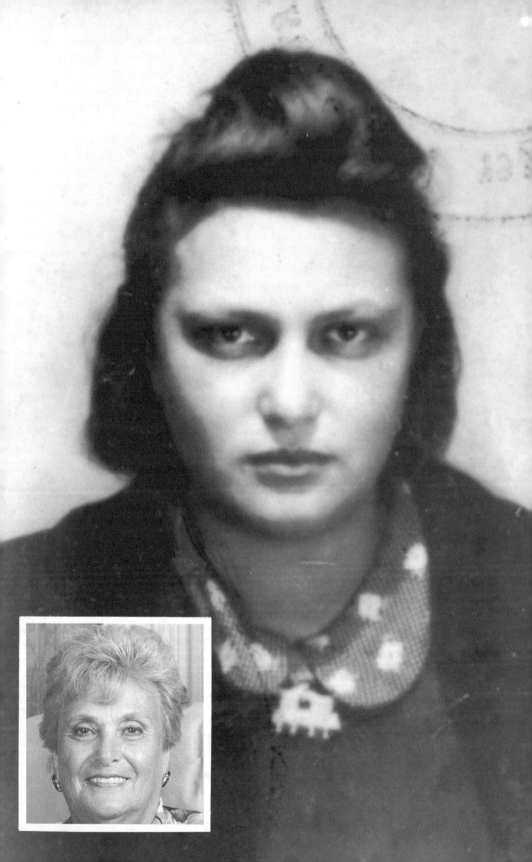

6

Henny Adler—Germany and Poland

"I was born in Berlin, Germany, in 1925 and was about eight years old when Hitler came to power. After he rose to a position of prominence, the lives of German Jews changed forever. All of a sudden, Christian boys and girls I'd always played with no longer wanted me near them. Now they called me cruel names and ran from me when I approached them.

"It was difficult to comprehend that this was really happening and even harder to deal with. For example, recess periods at our school were usually spent on the playground. When it was time to return to the building, we were expected to choose a partner with whom to walk quietly back into the classroom. One day when my Jewish friend was absent, I asked a Christian girl I used to play with if she wanted to be my partner. She looked at me ragefully and said, 'I'm not going to touch your hand, you're just a dirty Jew.' I was so hurt by her words that without thinking I slapped the girl across the face.

"Our school's principal, a very nice woman who I don't think was a Nazi yet, called my parents to school to discuss the incident. The other girl's parents were in touch with school authorities as well. It was decided that if I apologized, the matter would be dropped.

"But I didn't want to apologize, and most of all I didn't want anyone to think of me as a dirty Jew or humiliate me with verbal taunts. My former friend had insulted me, and although I knew it was wrong to hit anyone, I wasn't sorry for what I'd done. Being so young, it was still impossible for me to understand how one day you could be liked and the next you were treated as garbage because of your religion. Even though I'd always loved that school, I told my parents that I never wanted to go back.

"The matter was finally settled by my being transferred to a Jewish school. But the school was fairly far away and there was no direct bus transportation there. Meanwhile, Hitler's popularity continued to affect our lives. My young friends and I always enjoyed going to the movies, but now boldly printed signs on the theaters read NO JEWS ALLOWED.

"I, along with one of my girlfriends, didn't look Jewish. We could have easily passed as Christians and gone to a movie theater in an area where no one knew us. After thinking about it for a while, we decided to try it. But once we approached the theater, we looked at one another and both of us knew we couldn't go through with it. We had too much pride as Jews to deny who we were. So movies, along with many other small childhood pleasures, were gone.

"As time passed, we lost more than we ever dreamed possible. On October 28, 1938, at five o'clock in the morning, a German storm trooper, the SS, and local police knocked loudly at the door of our home. These men had come to arrest my father. We didn't know why this was happening, as my father hadn't done anything wrong. But we soon learned that he was being deported to Poland. Even though I was born in Germany, my parents originally came from Poland, and all adult males of Polish descent were being involuntarily returned to the land of their birth.

"Things became progressively worse. Soon afterwards my mother was made to do daily forced labor. We also had to give up our apartment so a Christian family could move in. All our furniture and possessions were confiscated as well. Now we were penniless except for some valuable jewelry my mother owned. Yet when she tried to sell the jewelry, she received barely a fraction of its true worth. As my mother and I walked back from the jeweler, we had to cross a bridge spanning a wide river beneath us. My mother felt so despondent that she contemplated jumping. But I clung to her coat and cried, begging her not to kill herself. After what seemed like an endless period of time, she agreed to walk home with me.

"My mother survived that day, but her life remained stressful. Now separated from my father, she felt completely responsible for her three children. Before long she mentally collapsed under the strain and couldn't continue functioning. Now she just lay in bed refusing all food and water. I remember kneeling at her bedside urging her to eat. For weeks I went to school without breakfast or lunch— my mother could hardly care for herself, let alone me.

"My mother finally emerged from her depression, and in July 1939 our family joined my father in Poland. Now we lived in the town of Tarnow where my parents and brothers were born. But less than two months after we settled in our new home, Germany invaded Poland. Soon my father was forced to work for the Nazis. I remember that my mother left her fur coat with a Gentile friend for safekeeping as well as hid a silver chandelier beneath our porch.

"By 1941, terror reigned in our city. At times SS men shot any Jew on sight, as though we existed for their target practice. Then on June 10, 1942, some Christian friends warned us that serious trouble was brewing. To prepare for what might happen, our mother instructed us to wear street clothes beneath our bedclothes that night.

"Sure enough, by five o'clock the next morning, we

51

heard a loud rapping on our door. Moments later, two SS were inside our home—one pointed a rifle at my head. Even though I was young and afraid of what might happen next, I managed to retain my composure. Speaking in German, I explained how I'd been born in Berlin and how both my parents now held jobs that were useful to the Third Reich. The men left our apartment.

"But my aunt, uncle, and young cousin who lived one floor beneath us were not as lucky. They were immediately dragged out to the courtyard and shot. We heard the gunfire from our apartment. Then the SS men left without realizing that my thirteen-year-old cousin was badly wounded, but still alive. He cried out for help, but instead of helping him, some Christian Polish people who lived in an apartment off the courtyard simply called the SS back to finish him off. Although my grandmother lived downstairs with my aunt, uncle, and cousin, she wasn't killed with the others. Instead, after being made to watch most of her family being murdered, she was put on a wagon filled with old people. All were taken to a nearby Jewish cemetery. After arriving, they were blindfolded and shot. These people were guilty of nothing more than being Jews. But during those times, that was comparable to a capital crime.

"Seeing a portion of my family murdered that way was one of the most traumatic experiences of my life. Even years later, I couldn't tolerate the sound of fireworks because it reminded me of the ripple of bullets that cut short the lives of my loved ones. Apparently there'd been quite a bit of killing that night. The next morning, as I walked through the streets, I had to step over bodies. That night was typical of others to come. So many Jews in our town were killed that before long our numbers were significantly reduced.

"Then, in the fall of 1942, the remaining Jews were crowded into a small area called a ghetto. The Germans surrounded the enclosure with barbed wire. To keep us from starving, my mother sold the few things she had left.

52

Some of the Christian Poles living near the ghetto were quite poor. On Sundays we'd see them going to church wearing faded clothing. My mother sold all her lovely silk and linen dresses to these farmers' wives in exchange for some potatoes and vegetables. From then on, we saw them attending Sunday services in those beautiful outfits.

"Since we weren't allowed out of the ghetto, we conducted our various business transactions through openings in the barbed wire fence enclosure. All sorts of goods were smuggled in and out of the ghetto this way. Still, the significant food shortage was difficult to rectify without ample funds. Although we'd never been rich before Hitler's reign, we were comfortable and always had enough to eat. One day I saw my mother crying and when I asked her why, she said it was because she only had a small portion of tapioca for the family. She knew how much my brother disliked tapioca, but now he could no longer afford to be a picky eater. I tried to make her feel better by eating my share of the tapioca and telling her that it tasted especially good. But I think she saw through my attempt to lighten her burden.

"Once, to celebrate a Jewish holiday with a proper meal, we exchanged my father's last suit for a small scrawny chicken. My mother prepared the meal and tried to stretch the meat to serve seven people. When I walked into the kitchen, I'd caught her standing over the sink licking the chicken bones. I asked her when she was going to eat, but she said she'd already eaten. I knew she was lying so the rest of us could have larger portions.

"In September 1942, the Germans conducted what was known as an 'action.' They ordered all older people living in the ghetto to report to a designated area for deportation. The age range indicated included my parents. We knew of a hiding place beneath our building's basement, and my brothers and I begged them to hide rather than report. But my father refused to do so. He was afraid the SS would kill his children in reprisal if they couldn't locate him. He

53

and my mother weren't willing to risk our lives. Before my mother left, she took off her wedding ring and said, 'This is the only thing I have left to sell. Use it in whatever way it will help you most.' As we said our goodbyes, I knew that was the last time I'd ever see my parents.

"I felt numb as I watched them walk away. But I hadn't much time to dwell on my feelings because the very next day the SS arrived at our apartment and announced that we all had to leave. We were to immediately report to the same area my parents had. They herded all the people from our ghetto into the street and made us run toward the destination. The SS fired their guns into the air as well as shot anyone who wasn't moving fast enough.

"For the past few days I'd been ill with an extremely high fever, and it was difficult for me to even walk, let alone run. So to save my life, my two brothers pulled my arms over their shoulders and carried my weight as they ran. If they hadn't been there to help me, I'm sure I would have been shot.

"After arriving, we stood in rows for hours while SS officers made their selections. Very young children and their parents were separated from the rest of us. We assumed that the children were probably going to be killed. They needed care and were too young to work or be useful to the Germans. And that day it seemed certain that their parents would be murdered along with them.

"To my amazement, I saw some parents actually push their own children away. I guess they knew they couldn't save them, so they tried to save themselves. It was hard for me to believe that a mother would run from her child, but evidently the fear of death can be overwhelming. Other people reacted quite differently. One young man I knew voluntarily picked up and carried his two-year-old nephew. Numerous people did the same. It was clear that they didn't want to go on living if their children were killed.

"Those of us who remained were moved to a smaller

ghetto. We were required to work for the Germans at a variety of jobs for which we received no pay. Since we labored outside the ghetto, each day we were marched to and from work under armed guard. The SS made us sing as we marched so that Christian onlookers would think we were well treated and in good spirits.

"During this period, I'd fallen in love with a Jewish boy named Morris. Morris and I planned to marry when we were older if we survived the war. Morris hadn't been with us in either ghetto. Instead, a Polish family had taken him in and he remained in hiding. Yet occasionally I'd still hear from him. We'd managed to exchange a few words through the ghetto's barbed wire fence. At times, I received letters from Morris through a third party. Knowing that one day we'd be together helped me keep my sanity. I had someone to live for.

"In September 1943, the Germans planned a final action which would nearly empty our ghetto. Most of us were to be shipped out. Morris somehow learned of their intentions and tried to help me. He thought that if he had some money he might be able to bribe someone and 'purchase' my safety for a while longer.

"Once they'd suspected serious trouble from the Nazis, both my mother and Morris's mother left some valuable silver and luxurious fur coats with two Christian Polish families. Our mothers believed these people were our friends and would keep the items for us until the war was over and we could reclaim them. Unfortunately, our parents had already been killed. So to save me, Morris went to these families and asked them for our goods, which he now hoped to sell for cash. But the families had come to enjoy our possessions and decided to give Morris up rather than the items. They told a Polish informer of his whereabouts and Morris was killed.

"I was subsequently shipped out with most of the others in the ghetto. We were packed into cattle cars and taken to a camp called Plashow. Although this was a work camp, they didn't have any real work for us while I was there. Instead they had us carry extremely heavy stones from place to place. There was also an infamous hill at Plashow known among camp inmates as the 'Hill of Death.' Nearly every night some people were taken there to be shot for some infraction of the rules.

"While I was at the camp, there was a widespread outbreak of scarlet fever. One of my brothers became extremely ill with the disease. When I'd secretly visit him in the infirmary, he'd beg me for something to drink. I stole a carrot and hoped to squeeze the juice from it to give to him. But an SS guard caught me where I shouldn't have been and kicked me so hard that my body spun across the ground. I was in terrible pain and left with a permanent back injury. But I didn't despair for two reasons—the SS guard hadn't shot me and I still had the carrot. I later managed to grate the carrot into a small cup of juice which I gave to my brother. I never saw him again after that.

"In December 1943, I was shipped from Plashow to a camp which supplied workers for an ammunition factory. Conditions were somewhat better there, as inmates were not generally killed unless they disobeyed. We worked from early morning until late afternoon. For sustenance, we were given a small bowl of clear soup and a cup of something that resembled coffee. Some of the men were so hungry that they'd lick drops of spilled soup from off the ground. We slept on the floor of a barracks that teemed with lice and rodents. One girl was badly bitten by a rat on her nose.

"From that camp, I was sent to another camp named Chenstochowa, which was situated in what was thought to be among the most anti-Semitic cities in Poland. There I worked in a camp factory testing bullets. My supervisor was a kind German man who saved my life on more than one occasion. He'd spoken up for me once after a German officer spotted me at the factory and decided that from then on I'd work for him. I knew his intentions as did everyone else. He had a reputation for having sex with young Jewish prisoners before killing them. But when the officer informed my supervisor that I'd be leaving the following day, he [my supervisor] insisted that I was too valuable to be transferred to another work detail. I was allowed to stay because of the firm stand my supervisor took.

"By December 1944, the war was beginning to wind down, although as prisoners it was difficult for us to keep track of events. Yet about that time an influx of SS officers arrived at our camp. I tried to listen carefully whenever I was around them and, as I spoke German, I understood what they said. I was horrified when I overheard their plans to send all of us to another camp to be gassed.

"One transport left our camp, and while another was loading, I begged my supervisor to help me. He secured permission for me to remain until the camp officially closed. Yet, as it happened, many more of us were saved because our liberation by Allied forces came in the form of a near miracle. Although we hadn't known it, even as the prisoner transports were loading, Russian troops were rushing towards our camp. The Allies feared the Germans might try to kill all camp survivors to eliminate possible witnesses who could later testify against them. Some of my camp friends were already tightly crammed into cattle cars and about to embark on their final train ride when the soldiers charged in. Those on the transport were saved—as I said, it was like a miracle."

7

Sam Adler—Poland

"When Hitler's soldiers first marched into our Polish town of Tarnow, there were no dramatic overnight changes. But within days the SS followed, and after that our lives were never the same. I'd been born in Poland and was a young man at the time of the invasion. I'd watched the SS pick up Jews off the street and force them to do their bidding.

"I happened to be out one day when I was spotted by an SS officer who beckoned me to him. As I hoped to avoid this encounter, I pretended I hadn't seen him. I dashed into a building which I knew had an exit on its other side through which I could leave. But the SS officer pursued me, and moments later he stood behind me pointing his revolver at my head while ordering me to stop. I knew if I ran I'd be dead. He immediately put me to work unloading and carrying in mattresses and various articles of furniture for the SS housing unit. In the months that followed, I experienced several similar incidents.

"Sensing that Polish Jews might soon find themselves in an extremely threatening predicament, I tried to think of

59

ways to protect myself. I was concerned about my family's safety as well. Poland was partitioned into two halves. One portion was controlled by the Russians, while the other side where my family lived was now occupied by German forces. I thought I'd be better off in the Russian-controlled zone. I had three brothers and I hoped two of them would accompany me. My parents felt my youngest brother would be safe with them since he was just eight years old. We never imagined that the Germans would routinely kill very small children.

"Even though I was the youngest of my remaining brothers, I was the most determined to leave. They eventually agreed to come along. My mother rented a horse and buggy to take us to the border. Crossing the Russian border was a high-risk endeavor. Since we weren't legally permitted to enter the Russian zone, there was always the possibility of being shot while running past the border guards.

"That evening, the Russians did shoot as we raced through the boundary markers, but luckily they only fired into the air to frighten us into returning home. Once we were safely in the Russian zone, I looked back and saw my mother still standing where we'd left her at the border. She'd wanted to see for herself that we were safe. I remember smiling when I saw the look of relief on her face. I hadn't known it then, but that was the last time I'd ever see her.

"Shortly after crossing the border, we were apprehended by Russian soldiers, who detained us overnight. They thought they'd receive orders in the morning to send us back, but we were permitted to stay. The three of us found work in a small town. Yet after two or three months my brother Morris became homesick and decided to chance returning home. We later learned that he managed to hide with a Christian Polish family until he was killed by an informer.

"My remaining brother and I stayed in the Russian zone, but after about seven months, things became increasingly complicated. The Russian government decreed that anyone from German-occupied Poland who wished to stay on would now have to become a Russian citizen. My brother, and some other refugees, were reluctant to do so, as they feared it might then be extremely difficult to return home following the war.

"But when we rejected their offer of citizenship, our Russian hosts retaliated. First, they tried to send us back to German-occupied Poland, but the Nazis refused to accept Jews. So instead the Russians sent us to a logging camp in Siberia [a cold, sparsely populated area of the Soviet Union.]

"It was hard labor in biting cold weather, but we were young, strong, and determined to survive. Even though we were Poles, we weren't treated any worse than Russian citizens sent to such camps for various violations. Anyway, before long things improved, as the Polish and Russian governments reached an agreement guaranteeing freedom for all Polish citizens held in Russian labor camps.

"Once freed, my brother and I were permitted to travel wherever we wished in Russia. By 1945, we'd heard that the war would soon be over and that there might be a way to safely return home. We journeyed to Moscow and from there hitched rides on trains wherever we could until we reached the Polish border.

"We'd finally returned home, but our worst fears were soon confirmed when we arrived at a formerly beautiful, nearly all-Jewish town called Baranowich. The sight that met my eyes sent shivers down my spine. The entire town was totally devastated. The people were gone and the magnificent buildings and homes had been burned down. Although we'd heard rumors of atrocities against Jews, I hadn't allowed myself to believe them. I'd tried to retain some hope, but seeing that town ended any pretense I might have clung to. Now I knew what had happened to my people.''

Author's note: After the war, Sam Adler fell in love with Henny—the young, pretty woman who'd been engaged to Sam's brother Morris before Morris's death during the Holocaust. Sam and Henny married and eventually came to America. Today they have three children and six grandchildren. Sam's love and caring were instrumental in Henny's recuperation from the serious back injury she sustained after being kicked by an SS officer.

The couple have done their best to put the Holocaust behind them, but at times their recollections become frighteningly real. As Henny Adler related: "During the war, I'd seen newborn babies torn apart limb from limb by German soldiers so as not to waste bullets on human beings small enough to be destroyed by hand. Years later, my doctor reported that while under anesthetic giving birth to my own child, I cried out, 'This is one baby the Nazis won't get!' The Holocaust may be over, but I don't know if all the pain and loss can ever be over for those of us who survived.''

8
Stefan Weinberg—Poland

"It started when I was sixteen years old and living with my family in Krakow, Poland. Our first inkling that trouble lay ahead came in September 1939 when we heard planes flying above us and explosions in the distance. Naturally, we thought we had only heard military maneuvers. No one in our neighborhood believed that war could actually break out, but within hours we realized we were mistaken.

"On September 6, we watched German soldiers march into the city. Normalcy ended the day they arrived, since their abuse of the Jewish population began immediately. As truckloads of invading German soldiers disembarked, they picked up Jews from off the streets and drove us to the outskirts of our city. We were made to remove the bodies and debris resulting from recent fighting in the vicinity. While some of us were allowed to return home, others were shot after completing their tasks. The Jews who escaped participation in this grisly chore were nonetheless at the Nazis' mercy. Often when German soldiers spied a Jew with a beard, they would call him over and

cut it off. Some even used their fists to pull out the individual's facial hair.

"Within weeks of the German invasion, Jews were confined to their homes. Soldiers stood outside with rifles pointed at our dwellings. If you stepped outdoors or came too close to a window, you would be shot. About that time, the looting started as well. We were made to stand in the hallway or outside while German soldiers entered our homes and took whatever they wished. Gold wedding bands as well as silver and brass items quickly disappeared as did other objects of value. As the looting raged, any Jew who happened to be standing in the vicinity might be randomly selected to receive a brutal beating.

"The Germans requisitioned the better homes and apartments of Polish Jews for their own use. The families living there were only given about ten minutes to gather a few belongings and leave. German soldiers carefully watched to ensure that they took nothing of value with them. In any case, they were only allowed to bring what they could carry. Fur coats and valuable art pieces were left behind for the Nazis.

"Before long, every Jew was required to sign in at a central registry. Then the various shops and stores owned by Jews were taken over by Germans. Regardless of whether you were young or old, you were now required to work for the Germans unless you were in a position to help them in another way. I worked for the German company Siemens Werke laying railroad tracks. I also unloaded provisions for German soldiers.

"You learned early on that Jews were treated as nonpersons. If they wished, the Nazis could work us till we dropped. A Jew might be forced to labor twenty-four hours a day or until a particular job was completed. During that time, we'd see two or three shifts of Germans come and go.

"We tried to continue on, but by 1941 the lives of Polish Jews had dramatically changed. An order was given requiring us to leave our homes within forty-eight hours and move to a small, sectioned-off slum area of the city called a ghetto. Our ghetto was encircled by a concrete wall with barbed wire, which we had to build ourselves within a seventy-two-hour period while patrolled by armed guards with attack dogs. Everyone instantly became a bricklayer. When portions of the wall weren't completed on schedule, selected workers were shot.

"You needed a special pass to either enter or exit the ghetto. Whole families were required to live together in a single room, so if a nine-room ghetto apartment was available, nine families resided there. We had a curfew, and after that hour were not allowed outside without a special permit.

"For about nine to ten months, ghetto families were generally allowed to remain intact. Then, in June 1942, the first deportation began. Several thousand people were shipped directly to Belzec, an extermination camp in eastern Poland. The deportations continued, and by the second week of June nearly half our ghetto's population had disappeared. Of course, at the time, we hadn't known that they'd gone to their deaths.

"There was little we could do to protect ourselves anyway. Even before all the ugliness began, my family had contemplated fleeing Poland. In fact, we secured visas to Palestine [now Israel]. But we didn't go because we didn't want to leave our other relatives behind. Besides, we never fully comprehended what could happen to all of us.

"Those of us who remained in the ghetto witnessed atrocities on a daily basis. One German SS officer seemed to enjoy randomly shooting Jews while strolling down our streets. He especially relished coming across women with infants or small children—then he'd aim for the smaller target. During this time, German soldiers evacuated a Jewish hospital. Patients who were able to walk were loaded onto a truck and taken away. Those needing assistance to move were shot in their beds. We began to hear accounts of how groups of Jews taken to deserted areas by Nazis were shot after being forced to dig their own graves.

"Before long, our ghetto was split into two sections— the working ghetto and the nonworking ghetto. Residents of the working ghetto labored daily at jobs for the Germans. Those in the nonworking ghetto remained available for various work projects which arose. At times, German soldiers would arrive at the nonworking ghetto and request fifty to one hundred Jews for a particular task. Sometimes these individuals returned, but on other occasions they did not.

"On March 13, 1943, our entire ghetto was liquidated. Those from the working ghetto were taken to Plashow, a concentration camp about six miles away. Plashow was a work camp rather than an extermination camp, yet eighty thousand Jews eventually died there. My mother was among those who died. While ill at the camp's infirmary, she was given a lethal injection.

"There were random killings at Plashow as well. Once a high-ranking SS officer attended the camp's morning roll call. For no particular reason, the officer pulled a young man from the line and shot him in the head with his revolver. An older man standing next to the deceased had remained silent as he watched the teenager die. If he'd spoken out, he'd have been shot as well. He exercised a great deal of self-control, because the dead boy was his son. But in spite of such incidents, Plashow inmates were thought to be fortunate. Jews from the nonworking section of our ghetto had been taken directly to Auschwitz, an extermination camp where they were killed immediately.

"I had been among those chosen to return to clean out our abandoned ghetto. Although a hundred and fifty of us had been taken to the work site from Plashow, the SS later determined that only seventy-five workers were needed. They lined us up and told every other person to step out. The man in front of me as well as the one behind me left the line. These extra workers were taken around the corner and shot.

"The remaining seventy-five of us set about the task of packing up the former ghetto residents' belongings. Their clothing and household articles were shipped to Germany. We also had to undress the corpses of the workers slain that day so their clothing could be shipped off as well. The clean-up project continued for months. Often as we emptied out the apartments, we'd find bits of food left behind in cupboards. Therefore, we sometimes had more to eat than many of the inmates.

"At times, German soldiers found families hiding out in the deserted ghetto. I was present once when this occurred. First, they marched the adults and older children out of the building. Then one of the soldiers tossed a baby out of a window several stories high. He shouted to another soldier below to catch it, but the other didn't even attempt to do so. Both men laughed at the sight of the infant's lifeless body splattered on the pavement, as one remarked, 'Oops, looks like I missed that Jew.'

"Generally, Jews found in hiding were instantly killed. While I was at Plashow, one of my cousins was brought to the camp. She tried to pass as a Christian but was found out. Somehow she escaped being shot, yet she wasn't allowed to live very much longer. Often transports of Plashow children were sent to extermination camps. Soon after her arrival, I heard an SS officer call my cousin to join the children being loaded onto the truck. I had two other cousins at Plashow, but there was nothing any of us could do to save her.

"After about seven months, the ghetto cleanup project was completed. Then once again I was chosen for another desirable camp assignment. A large amount of clothing, furniture, and other items confiscated from Jewish families was brought to Plashow. I was among those who worked sorting and packing the items for shipment to Germany. But when that task ended, my next job was considerably less pleasant. All the concentration camp inmates were made to dig up the mass graves of those killed at Plashow. After we finished digging, we had to lift the bodies from the graves so they could be burned. The SS wished to leave no visible trace of their sinister activities.

"Once the dead were burned, I, along with many others, was packed into a cattle car and taken to a camp on the German border named Gross Rosen. It was one of the worst camps in existence. As soon as we arrived, some of us were pushed and beaten while others were shot. Although it was quite cold at the time, we were made to undress outdoors and stand in line naked. Close by was a man-made lake in which some naked, shivering people stood. I believe they were part of a Nazi medical experiment.

"The living conditions were abominable. Inmates slept so tightly packed together that you were forced to lie on your side. Every few hours, at the guard's command, we had to turn over, but it wasn't always easy to do so. If the person next to you died during the night, you had to turn his body over before turning yours. If you didn't act immediately on command, you might be beaten to death or taken outside and shot.

"From Gross Rosen I was taken on an eight-day train ride to a camp called Buchenwald. As soon as you arrived at Buchenwald, you were required to learn the camp song sung by inmates as they marched. Those caught not singing were severely beaten. Buchenwald's SS officers had inquired who among us were metal tradesmen. Although I hadn't worked in that industry, I told them I had. I felt my chances of survival would be improved if the Germans thought I might be of use to them.

"In December 1944, the metalworkers were sent to the Black Forest area not far from the Rhine River in Sonneberg, Germany. There, nearly six hundred of us produced gears for German V2 rockets. I worked in a group with two friends. To survive in a concentration camp, you

69

needed friends. Those who were really alone were much more likely to die. While there we learned from the others that every five to six months about ninety-five percent of the prisoners were shipped back to Buchenwald, where they were immediately killed. The remaining five percent stayed on to train the new incoming prisoners and perform other duties.

"Our work group was required to make six gears a day. Once when I accidentally produced a malfunctioning part, I was well aware of the possible consequences. Depending on the guard's mood, I might either receive fifty lashes or be shot. However, the Germans didn't know that a few weeks earlier I, along with a friend from our group, had found a way to produce the gears nearly twice as fast as was required. My friend thought our overseer might be pacified if we produced two additional gears above our daily quota. I agreed it was worth a try, but since I thought my life might be at stake, I decided to produce four instead of two extra gears.

"At day's end, the factory manager could scarcely believe what we'd accomplished. He measured all the pieces and announced that each was perfect. I explained that while improving the assembling process I'd accidentally produced a defective part, but he was so thrilled with the four extra gears that he told me not to worry. From then on, I was also permitted to go to the German kitchen for leftovers each evening. Since the Germans at our factory ate well, I had enough food to share with my twelve bunkmates.

"Our camp wasn't far from the Rhine River, and one morning we heard gunfire coming from that direction. We realized that the Allies had to be near, and within hours, the SS began to evacuate our camp. This time there weren't any trains or truck transports—we were to walk. Although I didn't know it, we were being taken on a death march.

"As we marched along the road, a number of inmates managed to escape. I, along with two of my friends, was among them. For about forty-eight hours we hid in a bombed-out house, but when we tried to move on, we had the misfortune of meeting up with a group of SS officers from our camp. They had us rejoin the others, but by then only about half the inmates had survived the march.

"I thought they would have killed us right off, but instead the SS officers decided to put us on a punishment detail. We were made to push a huge carriage filled with provisions for the SS. As we walked, different guards took turns slamming their gun butts into our ribs every few minutes. After a few days, I was so badly bruised that I didn't think I could continue. One of the friends I'd run away with helped me up and tried to support a greater portion of the load we pushed.

"Since I felt certain that I probably wouldn't survive the punishment detail, my friends and I began to look for a way to escape again. That night as we camped near a farm, the three of us slipped away, again using darkness as our cover. We ran to the farmer's barn and quietly hid in the hay. Nearly a dozen other prisoners followed our lead and hid in the same barn. But before long the guards realized we were missing and began to search for us. After finding the barn where we hid, they used bayonets and pitchforks to poke around in the hay for us. One of their bayonets missed my face by inches. Before long, some of those in hiding were discovered. They were mercilessly beaten before being shot.

"Then one of the SS loudly suggested that those of us who remained in hiding come out voluntarily. As an inducement to do so, he promised that we would be shot immediately and escape the beating. Those who accepted his offer were quickly taken outside the barn. We heard the gunfire that killed them from where we hid. Then, suddenly, one of the friends I'd run away with panicked. He said we ought to give ourselves up, stressing that at least we'd escape being tortured before dying. Afraid that the sound of his voice might reveal our position, I clasped my hand over his mouth and forcefully held it there. I hoped I wasn't suffocating him, because after a time he looked as if he was about to turn blue. I wanted to save my friend, not kill him. After the Germans left, he was fine and very glad to be alive.

"We remained in that barn until nightfall. Then the two of us headed for the forest, where we walked for days before coming upon a Polish camp. This was a Polish workers' camp, not a concentration camp. People remained there freely while employed at local farms and orchards. My friend and I decided to try to pass as Christian Poles. Because we were Jewish, we spoke Yiddish—the language used by Eastern European Jews. However, while living in Poland, I had perfected my Polish. Yet since my friend spoke Polish with a Yiddish accent, we had to pretend he was mute while I spoke for us both.

"It was important to continually keep up a pretense because no one could be trusted. Being an escaped Jew was worse than being a hunted animal. Some people kill animals for food or even for sport. But a Jew might be killed simply because he was a Jew.

"The Polish workers allowed us to stay with them. They gave us Bibles and large crosses, which we tried to keep in plain sight whenever we thought someone might be eyeing us suspiciously. We traveled to the next town, Buchau, with our Polish work group, but there we came across a roadblock in the town's center staffed by German state police. They shouted, 'Papers, papers.' We were required to show our identification papers, and although my friend and I wore crosses and carried Bibles, we had no such documents.

"As a result, we were arrested and taken to an empty schoolhouse. Several Russian and Greek laborers had been taken there as well. Before long, a German major who spoke several languages arrived. When he spoke to us in German, I'd say I didn't understand, again relying on my perfect Polish accent. As German is quite similar to Yiddish, I'd learned to speak it fairly well and knew precisely what he said. Yet I thought he might be trying to trick us to see if we knew Yiddish and were therefore Jews. The major spoke to us at length and in several languages, but never accused me of being a Jew. Yet before leaving he stepped back, took a long, hard look at me, and said, 'I still don't believe you are a Pole.'

"After he left, a guard took us to the local Gestapo office in the next town. Even though the war was practically over, the Gestapo still remained. When a Gestapo officer led us behind a curtain, I thought we'd be killed. I felt certain he'd make me drop my pants to see if I'd been circumcized. Back then Jewish men were usually circumcized while few European Christians were.

"Instead, he told me to roll up my right sleeve and raise my arm. I realized he was looking for the number tattooed on concentration camp inmates. I didn't have a tattoo because the Germans hadn't bothered tattooing prisoners they intended to send directly to extermination centers. They considered it a waste of effort and ink to count someone they were about to kill. Since I'd been slated to go to an extermination center prior to having lied about being a metal tradesman, I'd never been tattooed. So when the Gestapo officer didn't see a number, he had no reason to believe I was Jewish.

"I, along with my friend, who also hadn't been tatooed, was released. Since we were thought to be Christians, we were eventually issued papers with Christian-sounding names. Equipped with the proper documents, we began our journey home. On the way back we met up with some American soldiers, who took us to a house where there was an abundance of food and comfortable beds. Yet at first I still slept on the floor, since I'd grown unaccustomed to the luxury of a bed.

"I eventually registered to come to America and am glad to be here, but the Holocaust remains an unerasable part of my past."

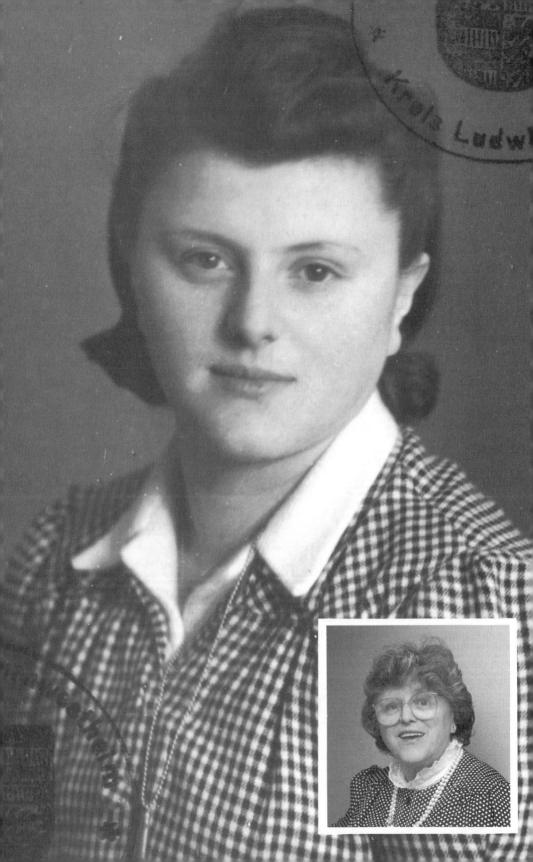

9
Sally Sander—Poland

"I was born in Bedzin, a Polish city near the German border. It had a population of nearly sixty-five thousand people, most of whom were Jewish. There were six people in my immediate family. I was the youngest of four children.

"When Germany attacked Poland in September 1939, the Polish army immediately fled from the area to evade the German soldiers. Our city's civilian population was left defenseless. My first encounter with German troops occurred on September 4, the very same day my older married sister went into labor with her first child.

"My mother sent me to get help, but the city was in chaos at the time, and it was impossible to locate a physician who'd come. I ended up fetching a midwife to assist in the birth, but our path to the apartment was blocked by the divisions of German soldiers marching through the city. I summoned up the courage to indicate to one of the officers in charge that I needed to cross the road, and fortunately he motioned us through with his rifle butt. Despite the turmoil, my sister successfully delivered a beautiful baby girl. At the time, we never imagined that just three years later this small Jewish child would be murdered by German soldiers.

"Yet actually, the slaughter of innocent people began almost immediately. My first personal encounter with it came shortly thereafter. While I was out on an errand for my mother, two strange men approached me and asked if I knew where a Jewish man named Hamburger lived. They said this man owned property in Berlin. But the only Mr. Hamburger I knew owned the stationery store where I bought my school supplies. Convinced that I couldn't help them, the men moved on. But a few days later, the man they sought was found shot. I saw his body leaning against our synagogue, where it had been propped up on some orange crates. The following day, that same synagogue was set on fire while religious services were being conducted. Many of the people worshiping inside were burned alive.

"Then the Gestapo took ten prominent Jewish businessmen, professionals, and intellectuals from our community as hostages. The rest of us were told that if we disobeyed their orders in any way, these men would be shot. First, the Gestapo requisitioned our valuables; then they later took our bicycles and radios.

"We felt as though our lives were being turned upside down. There were sporadic random killings. You'd hear of someone you knew being shot or of a neighbor who was taken away and did not come back. One day my oldest sister's husband went for a walk but didn't return. He'd been picked up by the Gestapo and sent away. We were later notified that the action occurred because he was a communist. My young brother-in-law knew nothing about communism—the main passion of his life had been skiing.

"As the months went by, increasing numbers of Jews began to disappear. Young men and women were picked up by the Gestapo to do physical labor. Frequently, night raids were conducted at Jewish homes. My mother was barely able to sleep most nights, since she always seemed to post herself at the door, hoping to somehow protect us. Gestapo tactics were notoriously ruthless. Suddenly, soldiers appearing in the middle of the night would use their boots and rifles to break down the doors of Jewish homes. They'd take away the family's able-bodied young adults to work for the Nazis.

"When we'd receive word of an impending raid, we were better able to protect ourselves. In one such instance, my mother hid me in a closet beneath a staircase and moved a dresser in front of the closet door. As anticipated, the soldiers broke in and quickly went through all the rooms. After looking around, they asked my mother if any teenage children were home. When she said no, they left without me.

"By that time, Jewish young people were no longer permitted to attend school. I'd always wanted to be a dress designer, but because I couldn't openly pursue my goal, my parents arranged for me to secretly study with some people in the fashion industry. Having acquired sewing and design skills, I was later of use to the Gestapo when individuals were needed to make uniforms for German flyers. Those of us with desired skills were able to buy some time before being sent to a labor camp.

"Nevertheless, your safety was never guaranteed. Every so often, all Jews were required to report to a large sports stadium in our area. There, German officers selected individuals for deportation. You could never be certain of when you'd find yourself on a transport. On July 22, 1942, my older brother, his wife and child, along with my older sister and I, reported to one of those stadium calls as we'd been instructed to do. The Nazis permitted me to go home, but my other family members never came back. I later learned that they were sent to an extermination camp where they were murdered.

"In January 1943, an area of the city called a ghetto

77

was set aside for Jews. All Jews were now forced to reside within these confines. As ghetto residents, we felt certain that one day soon the Nazis would come for us. So we decided to build an underground bunker, which was actually little more than a hole in the ground dug sufficiently large and deep enough to allow several people to stand in it together. Its trapdoor entrance was concealed by the large portable closet we placed over it. We thought of our bunker as a necessary measure and knew that other Jewish families constructed similar underground hiding places.

"Since our ghetto apartment was positioned so you could see some distance away, our family members took turns posting themselves as lookouts at the window. The day my sister spied Nazi tanks heading for the ghetto, we quickly ran to alert the other families. Then we began our descent into the bunker. Meanwhile, we saw a neighbor with a small child in her arms running towards her bunker. My mother realized that the woman would never reach it in time, so she called out to her to join us.

"As all of us stood closely together in the darkened dugout, we could hear German soldiers above us rounding up our friends and neighbors. When they entered our apartment, they couldn't find anyone home. But just when we thought they were about to leave, our neighbor's baby started crying. At that moment, we knew it was over. The sound of the baby's cries led the Nazis to our hiding place. They threw an ignited newspaper down into the hole to force us out.

"From there we were taken to the train depot and shoved into cattle cars. The traveling conditions were intolerable, and many passengers died along the way. I remember envying the dead. At least for them, all the pain and terror was over. Those of us who lived could only imagine what was ahead.

"When we arrived at the Auschwitz camp, SS officers began to separate us. Young mothers and children were

Auschwitz

sent in one direction, old people in another, while healthy young adults went still another way. I wanted to remain with my mother, but she insisted that I go with the other young people. Then the old people, very young children, and pregnant women were loaded onto trucks and driven away. My mother, father, and three-year-old niece were among them. My pregnant cousin, who'd arrived on the same transport, was taken with them as well.

"I, along with those who remained, was sent into the camp itself. As I walked toward its interior, I remember looking back and seeing the bright crematorium fires against the dark night sky. These fires blazed day and night, but even after arriving at Auschwitz, we still didn't realize what they were for.

"Many of the new Auschwitz inmates were anxious to learn where their friends and relatives were taken. We thought there might be special camps for the elderly and children, where the work was less strenuous. But when we questioned the inmates who'd been at Auschwitz for a time, they laughed at our naïve assumption and said, 'Look at those fires. Those are your parents and your little sisters and brothers.' We didn't want to believe what they said, but it was true.

"At Auschwitz I was assigned to work outside digging ditches. We dug in the freezing cold and rain, wearing only the thin, striped dresses issued to us. The ditches weren't to be used for any particular purpose; the Nazis were merely trying to work us to death. And many did die of sickness, cold, exhaustion, and starvation.

"Although I became very ill with typhus, I tried to continue working. I was afraid I'd be put to death if the Nazis knew how sick I was. But my condition worsened until I was barely able to move. Then I was taken to the camp's hospital, which was actually only a room to which people were sent to die. We weren't given any food or water. Female Jewish inmates who happened to be doctors supervised the unit, but without any medical supplies and equipment, they were unable to help us. Yet miraculously, I somehow improved on my own. Before long, I was able to stand and even walk a short distance. I tried to keep as active as I could because I knew that sometimes SS officers visited the hospital to send the very ill patients to the gas chambers.

"The health of the women in our hospital became especially relevant when we learned that SS officer Dr. Josef Mengele would soon be inspecting our unit to make selections. Dr. Mengele was a sadistic Auschwitz doctor who'd conducted inhumane medical experiments on inmates. He'd also earned a reputation among Jews for his brutality and the pleasure he appeared to take in sending people to their deaths.

"The night before he was to come, I saw at least a dozen girls crying and begging the Jewish inmate doctor in charge to save them. But their conditions had so deteriorated there was nothing she could do to disguise the seriousness of their illnesses.

"Although I'd improved, I still had a bad rash on my body from the disease. Someone smuggled in some white flour which we used to try to cover our rashes and sores. But it wasn't very helpful—you could see right through the thin layer of powder. However, my life was saved by a Christian Polish girl who, before being sent to Auschwitz, had been a medical student. The Nazis sent her, along with other Christian intellectuals who disagreed with their philosophy, to concentration camps. Due to her medical background, she'd been assigned to work with the doctor at our unit.

"I'd never even spoken to this woman, yet she took it upon herself to save me. She came over to me and said, 'My dear child, you're getting better. You can't afford to be here when Mengele comes tomorrow.' She took away the lice-infested blanket I'd wrapped around myself and

81

replaced it with a clean one. Then she spoke to the Jewish doctor on my behalf. The doctor decided I was well enough to return to the standard barracks, which I did immediately. I was lucky to be spared. But most of my ailing friends didn't fare as well. The following day they were gassed and their bodies burned.

"I had various other jobs at Auschwitz. One involved pushing a very large, heavy garbage truck around the camp to collect refuse. It took eight girls to push that truck, and as we walked we were followed by SS guards with dogs. If you didn't push the truck fast enough, the dogs were turned loose on you. Once my foot accidentally became caught beneath one of the truck's wheels. The pain seemed unbearable, and I still have a scar from that accident.

"In January 1945, as the Allied forces were nearing the camp, the SS decided to evacuate the prisoners. We were made to walk to another camp. We walked for three days and three nights. It was bitter cold and the icy ground was slippery, but we marched on in our torn shoes, thin, striped dresses, and light sweaters. If you weren't able to walk quickly enough and slipped toward the rear, a guard would shoot you. If you stumbled and fell along the way, you'd also be shot. To worsen our predicament, we weren't given any food as we traveled.

"We finally reached a camp called Ravensbrück near Berlin, Germany. The Allies were bombing Berlin, and as a result a great deal of disorganization had ensued. The camp SS didn't have time to assign us to barracks, so the first night we slept out in the snow. The following night a large number of women were crammed into a room. We had no space to lie down or even sit, so we slept standing up with one person leaning against another.

"I only remained at Ravensbrück for about six weeks. Since the Allies were nearly upon us, we were taken to another camp further north. Several months later, American soldiers liberated us. Even though I was finally free of the Nazis, it was hard to believe that somehow the SS wouldn't be back to kill us. After the Allies opened the camp gates, I didn't move for three days. I was exhausted, heartsick, and finding it difficult to believe that it was over. But it was over. Finally over."

Author's note: Sally Sander later married Zelik Sander, a boy she'd known before the war. The two eventually came to America to begin a new life.

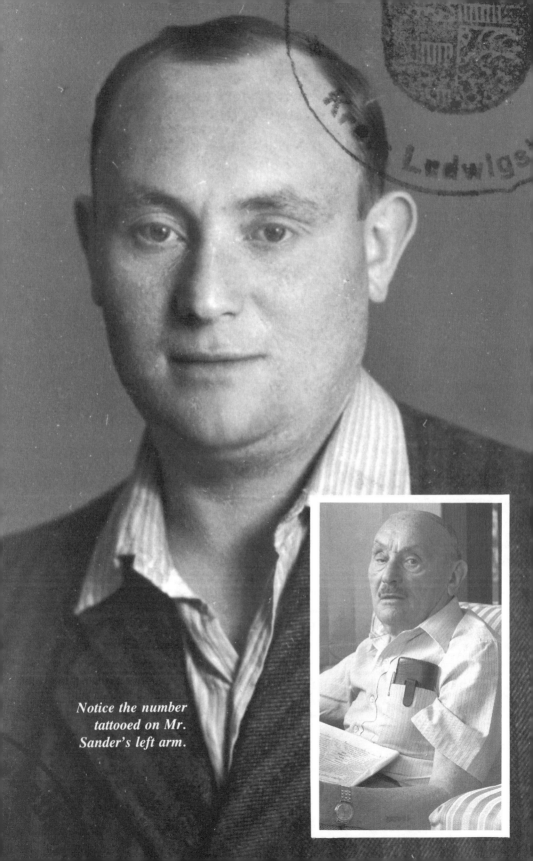

Notice the number tattooed on Mr. Sander's left arm.

10
Zelik Sander—Poland

"I was a newly drafted young Jewish soldier in the Polish army when the Germans invaded my country in September 1939. Shortly thereafter, I was captured by German soldiers and held in the prisoner-of-war camp Stalag 8. While detained, Jewish soldiers were not treated as well as our Christian counterparts, but we were nevertheless not beaten and starved as Jews in concentration camps were.

"When I was eventually released and returned home, I was shocked at the devastation that had taken place. Our synagogue, along with a row of Jewish homes and apartment buildings behind it where my family lived, had been destroyed. Now only about half of our apartment house stood. My family tried to continue living in the one room of our apartment which still existed.

"It didn't take long to realize that it would be difficult for a Jew to survive in Nazi-occupied Poland. Since my father's shoe store had been closed down by the Nazis, I now secretly sold shoes to both Jews and Christian customers. There was a degree of risk involved in these exchanges, but we had to survive somehow.

"As was the fate of so many Polish Jews, I was later sent to a ghetto, from which I was eventually transported to Auschwitz. There we lived with insects and dirt. Since all our blankets were lice-infested, we were elated when the guards announced that we'd have an opportunity to shower.

"After showering, we still had to use the same filthy blankets. But we felt lucky to have returned, since some of the inmates who'd gone to the showers didn't come back. They'd been taken to the showers next to the crematorium where they were gassed. Several weeks later when the Nazi guards inquired again if anyone would like a shower, no one volunteered.

"I remained in Auschwitz until January 1945 when the SS evacuated the camp to avoid the approaching Russian troops. After a three-day march, during which any person who collapsed or faltered along the way was shot, we were pushed into open cattle cars and taken for a freezing three-day train ride in the dead of winter. We arrived at the Buchenwald concentration camp, and after several days were transferred to a camp called Cravinkel about twenty miles from Buchenwald.

"The Germans stored munitions at Cravinkel, and each day the Jewish inmates unloaded the trucks bringing in shipments of various supplies. While at the camp I became friendly with a boy named Sigmund, and we decided that if we were marched to another camp, we'd try to escape. Relying on my previous army experience, I devised an escape strategy. When the time was right, we'd dash out from the column of marchers, run into the woods, and lie flat on the ground to avoid detection. A whistle would be the unspoken signal we'd use to find one another after the marchers had passed.

"When it was time for us to return to Buchenwald, the SS decided that we'd walk the twenty miles. We began the march in April 1945 during a tremendous downpour. When Sigmund saw the guards weren't looking, he seized the opportunity to bolt out of line into the woods. Shortly thereafter, I did the same.

"Although the Germans fired several shots at us, I wasn't hit. Once the marchers passed and the SS officers were out of sight, I whistled to Sigmund as we'd agreed to do. But when there was no response, I supposed he'd been killed by an SS bullet.

"I wandered alone in the woods for several days. I had to eat grass and other forest vegetation to stay alive. But I knew liberation was near, and I was determined to survive. Yet I was still extremely aware of being an escaped Jew in enemy territory. I didn't dare allow any of the local people to see me. Now I had to live by my wits, and a miscalculation could cost me my life.

"At one point I was startled by a rustle of leaves, indicating that someone was heading in my direction. To my immediate relief, I discovered that three other escaped prisoners had also sought asylum within the forest's camouflage. We walked together for a while before coming upon an empty house that was well stocked with food and provisions.

"Although no one was there at the time, it was obvious that before long the occupant would return. I devised a plan whereby three of us would sleep while one stayed up to act as a lookout. When the lookout spotted the owner, he was to wake the others, so that the four of us could jump the civilian before he had a chance to kill us or turn us in.

"But things didn't go as I'd hoped. When the German who owned the house returned, the lookout panicked. Instead of waking us, he ran from the house into the night. The German civilian was armed, and he fired at the fleeing man's back, killing him. Startled by the turn of events, the rest of us ran out the open door towards the woods. As we ran, the German fired at us as well.

"Moments later I was back in the woods, lying on the ground while hiding. Before long I got up and made my way deeper into the forest. After walking aimlessly for about ten days, I came to a clearing where I noticed some people whom I was unable to identify. Not wishing to take any chances, I hopped into a nearby ditch to conceal myself. But I'd already been noticed, and moments later I found myself confronted by several uniformed soldiers.

"The men pressed me for information about who I was and where the German soldiers were headed. I knew nothing of the SS's latest maneuvers, and by then I was much more interested in where the nearest piece of bread was. Although I didn't know it at the time, the men I spoke to were American soldiers.

"After I somehow convinced them that I was not the enemy, I was taken to a camp where a number of Jews were gathered. People all around me were relating their experiences to one another. There was someone there telling how his best friend, Zelik, helped him to escape during a march from a camp. Amazingly, my young friend Sigmund survived after all and arrived at the same camp!

"Having been liberated, I was technically free to roam the countryside, but the area hadn't yet been normalized. On one occasion, I, along with three other Jews, was mistaken for a German and ordered by American soldiers to unpack truckloads of their food. After years of suffering, deprivation, and hunger, completing this chore was difficult for us. Each man pilfered some items as he worked. An American officer guarding us noticed what we'd done and called us over. I told him in Yiddish [the language of Eastern European Jews] that we were hungry, and explained what our actual experiences had been.

"To our good fortune, the American soldier whom I'd spoken to was Jewish and understood Yiddish. His name was Captain Walter Rapp, and he'd actually been born in Germany and had come to the United States when he was younger. Once he found out who we were, he asked the GIs who ordered us to work, 'Haven't these people suffered enough?' Then he told them to find some German soldiers to put to work.

"The four of us traveled with Captain Rapp and his unit to the town of Kornwesttheim near Stuttgart, Germany. There Captain Rapp told me he'd been ordered back to the States and wouldn't be able to do any more for us. Yet prior to leaving, he introduced the four of us to the German mayor of the town, who happened to be anti-Nazi. Captain Rapp told the mayor to look out for us and mentioned that despite his present departure, he'd soon be returning to Germany. He really didn't know if he'd be back, but he wanted to be certain the mayor kept his word.

"Even after he'd left Europe, Captain Rapp continued to assist me. He'd inquired if I'd had relatives in America, and when I answered affirmatively, he asked his own family to track them down. After numerous letters and phone calls, they finally located my granduncle. Finding my relatives in the States was the first step in paving the way for my eventual arrival in America. In March 1947, my new wife and I set foot on U.S. soil for the first time. This has been our home ever since."

11
Ilse Loeb—Austria

"I was thirteen years old and living with my parents and brother in Vienna, Austria, when the Germans invaded our country in March 1938. The day after their arrival, Jewish businesses were vandalized and looted. The Nazis broke into a large Jewish department store in our neighborhood and wildly tossed merchandise from the doors and windows. Others with carts waited below to take the goods away.

"In the summer of 1938, the SS came to my father's printing business and told him to get out. Their takeover of our livelihood was as simple as that. Without his work, my father suddenly had nothing to do. He'd spend much of his time standing across the street from his old shop staring at what once was his. A large swastika was painted on the window. Now my father's involvement with the establishment was reduced to gazing at the building from a distance. It broke my heart to watch him, but there was nothing any of us could do.

"We also had to move out of our lovely apartment in a building we lived in for years. Our home was near a park

*Ilse Loeb with her parents in a park
near their home in Austria*

I enjoyed, but now a sign at the park's entrance read NO JEWS ALLOWED.

"My parents knew we had to leave Austria. As they were especially concerned with their children's safety, our departure became their first priority. They contacted a cousin in Holland who worked with a children's relief group to bring me across the border. I arrived in Amsterdam, Holland, in November 1938 and was placed with a lovely Jewish foster family with whom I stayed for nearly two years. Hitler hadn't yet invaded Holland, so our lives were pleasant, and I was able to remain in touch with my parents. My parents couldn't leave Austria, although they'd also tried to come to Holland. Once the Nazis learned that my father was a skilled printer, they wouldn't let him go, and instead forced him to print counterfeit money for them.

"When Germany invaded Holland in May 1940, I knew I had escaped to the wrong country. I'd have to endure Nazi persecution for a second time. At first, the activities of Jews were restricted, and later they began to hold raids to seize Jews for deportation. In June 1942, I received a letter from the Nazis indicating that I was to report to the railroad station for deportation to a German labor camp. Interestingly, Anne Frank's sister received the same letter the same day I did. It was then that the Frank family decided to go into hiding, and I did as well.

"Although my cousin who helped bring me to Holland was an Austrian Jew, he was blond and looked very Aryan. My cousin successfully passed as a Christian during the war. He was engaged to a Christian woman named Nicky, whom he couldn't marry because Jews weren't permitted to marry Christians. So when it was decided that I should go into hiding, my cousin's fiancée rented a house for all of us in an outlying suburb of Amsterdam. The house belonged to a Jewish couple who were nationally known musicians, but had to go into hiding themselves. As Nicky was Christian, everything was in her name and therefore perfectly legal. So my cousin and Nicky posed as a married Christian couple while I remained hidden within their home. If anyone saw me and inquired as to who I was, I was supposed to have been their young Christian maid.

"I couldn't leave the house during the day because we never knew who might be watching and become suspicious. Sometimes, after dark, I'd step into the fenced-in backyard for a few minutes to breathe some fresh air. After remaining with Nicky and my cousin for a few months, it grew too dangerous for me to stay any longer, so I was taken to a new hiding place. Now I hid in Nicky's parents' apartment.

"There I had to be especially careful because living so close to others in an apartment building made secrecy difficult. If Nicky's parents were out, I couldn't flush the toilet or turn on a light. While in hiding, I lived from hour to hour. My whole life revolved around not being caught, so I never really relaxed. I didn't have time to think about many things, because I had to concentrate on every move I made. For example, whenever I walked through a room, I had to remember never to step too near a window because someone might see me from the street or from another building.

"During the time I resided with Nicky's parents, one of Nicky's sisters married. A two-day wedding celebration was held at the bride's parents' home. They felt the groom wasn't to be trusted, so the family concealed my presence from him. For those two days I had to stay shut away in a small room in the apartment that no one knew about. Nicky's parents slipped food to me under the door. Although many guests were invited to the wedding reception, no one guessed that I was there.

"While I remained with Nicky's parents, I never left their apartment. Even stepping outside the building for a few seconds was unthinkably dangerous. Whenever guests came, I'd tiptoe to my secret room. But while I was there, I developed a bad cough that made things more difficult. I

94

had to suppress my cough whenever guests or delivery people came to the apartment.

"A few months later, the political situation in the suburb where Nicky and my cousin stayed improved, and Nicky felt it was safe for me to return. Being isolated in the suburbs had its advantages. I could occasionally breathe some fresh air, and Nicky helped me recover from my very bad cough. Yet although things were a bit better there, it wasn't an easy period for any of us. There was a food shortage and we were always hungry.

"Although the Germans forbade Dutch residents to hear foreign broadcasts, sometimes we'd go into the attic and secretly listen to foreign news reports on a small crystal radio. Those broadcasts gave us all courage, since the Germans propagandized that they were winning the war and that the Allies were near defeat.

"Unfortunately, our suburb elected a Dutch Nazi mayor who was determined to hunt down Jews for deportation. He devoted nearly all his evening hours to ferreting out those in hiding. Although the Dutch police largely disagreed with his politics, they had to accompany him on these raids. We had no advance warning of when they were coming, but we had a long driveway, and when cars approached I'd race to my hiding place in the attic. Once when they came to our residence, a Dutch policeman only had time to say one word to Nicky when she opened the door. He just said, 'Hide!' I was lucky—I wasn't found that night.

"There were other dangerous encounters as well. One day, the famous Jewish musicians from whom we rented the house knocked on our door and asked if they could spend the night. They couldn't remain at their former hiding place any longer and had nowhere to go. Having them with us was extremely dangerous, since they were well known throughout the neighborhood and might easily be recognized. But we couldn't turn them away.

"Later that evening, the woman looked adoringly at

the elegant living room piano on which she had previously practiced for her concerts. She walked over to it and lovingly touched its keys. Then she began playing a Mozart piece. Her husband took out his violin and accompanied her. It was the most beautiful music I ever heard, but when they finished we realized what a risk we had taken. Someone could have heard them playing and called the police. There was even a Dutch Nazi now living across the street.

"At times, anyone in hiding might do something impulsive, but that short concert could have cost us all our lives. Their playing went unreported, but the danger continued. The musician couple was unable to find a new hiding place the next day and stayed with us for nearly three weeks.

"By 1944, we were notified by the Dutch underground that our suburb was again becoming increasingly unsafe for Jews. Nicky learned of a wonderful couple, Mr. and Mrs. Vos, who, during the course of the war, had hidden thirty-two Jews. Taking me in meant putting their lives and the lives of their four children at risk, but they did so without question. They were an unusually courageous couple.

"To provide their clandestine guests with an emergency escape route, the Voses dug a tunnel beneath their house leading to the adjacent outdoor field. Whenever we were warned that the Nazis might be coming to look for Jews, I'd sleep outside, hidden in the dark field. I spent many nights outdoors hoping to remain undetected.

"By September 1944, things sufficiently settled to allow me to return to Nicky's and my cousin's house. We managed to survive an extremely cold winter without fuel, electricity, or very much food. Then we heard that before long the war would be over. Surprisingly, I wasn't elated over the news. I strongly suspected that my parents had been killed, and I wasn't ready to face that yet. My older brother had established himself in America and tried to bring our parents to the United States, but I knew he didn't succeed. After the war, I learned that my worst fears were true. Both my parents had been gassed by the Nazis.

"I contacted my brother, and by June 1947 I arrived in America. My brother lived in Chicago and that's where I met my husband. We moved to New York and had four wonderful children. Years later in 1988, I attended a conference in Washington, D.C., entitled Faith in Humankind. The State Department sponsored this event to honor Christian rescuers who'd saved Jews during the Holocaust.

"During one of the conference workshops, I overheard a man who was interviewing a woman sitting near me for a book he was writing. He asked her, 'How were you able to jeopardize your own life and the lives of your family to save so many people?' Then I heard a familiar voice answer, 'I did what I had to do, that's all.' I turned around to see the woman who spoke, and there sat Mrs. Vos."

Author's Note: Ilse Loeb learned that the Voses now lived in upstate New York. She renewed her friendship with the Vos family and was pleased to find that they had received numerous humanitarian honors. When Mr. Vos died in 1990, Ilse Loeb spoke at his funeral. Today her special bond and friendship with Mrs. Vos continues.

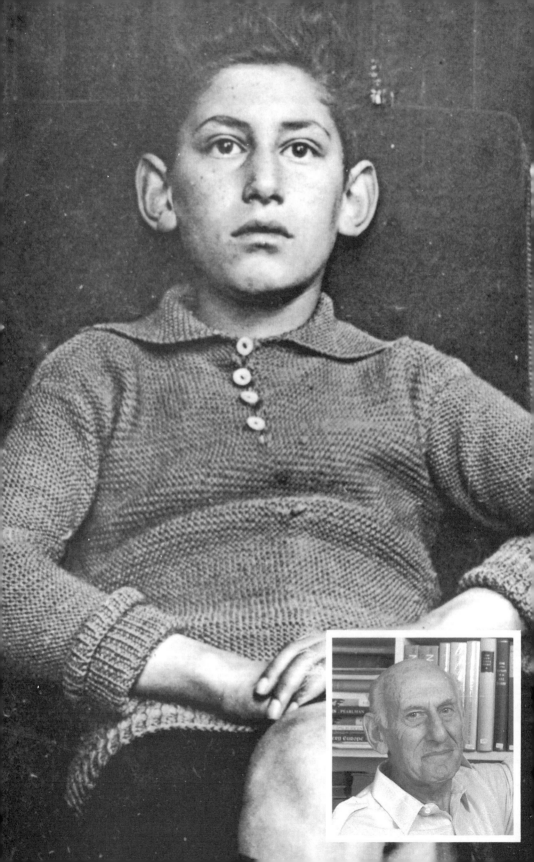

12

Jack Polak—Holland

"By July 1942 the Nazis in Holland schemed to perpetuate the myth of 'good Jews' and 'bad Jews.' The good Jews were those who followed Nazi dictates, adhered to imposed curfews, wore a yellow star, and permitted their possessions to be confiscated. Gestapo officers assured these good Jews that no harm would come to them. They were merely going to labor camps where they'd be well treated for their efforts.

"Yet it was very easy for even a 'good Jew' to die at the Nazis' hands. Anyone walking down the street with a yellow armband was considered easy prey. If you passed a German soldier, he might say, 'Why are you looking at me, Jew?' If he didn't care for your reply, you could be shot right there. If, on the other hand, you looked down at the ground when passing a German, he could just as easily yell out to you, 'Jew, why are you looking away from me?' and kill you with a comparably righteous attitude.

"By July 1942, the Germans had begun the deportation of Dutch Jews to labor camps. As in every European country the Nazis had invaded, the first Jews to go were poor people. The middle class followed and lastly the wealthy. At times, individuals of high status in the community might be allowed to remain at home a bit longer. Yet in the end nothing helped—everyone was deported.

"Each week a transport of Jews was taken from their hometowns to a Dutch transit camp called Westerbork. Then from Westerbork further deportations began to what were supposedly labor camps. We didn't learn that some of these labor camps were actually killing centers until the war was nearly over.

"My family managed to remain in Amsterdam, Holland, until July 1943. But it was hardly a peaceful existence as our lives were filled with fear. We hesitated to go to sleep at night because the Gestapo could come for us at any time.

"Terror soon became a familiar feeling. At times, the Germans held special raids. Once they rounded up about four hundred Jews, picking up anyone with a yellow star off the street. That time I was among those taken. They marched us through the streets of Amsterdam before selecting ten out of the four hundred, whom they shoved up against the wall. I happened to also be one of the ten. Ten SS men immediately came forward with their guns drawn and stood in front of us. I thought my life was over, but instead of shooting us, they shot into the air. To this day, I don't know why we weren't killed then and there.

"After the false firing, we were marched to a schoolhouse where all four hundred of us were questioned and photographed. Out of the four hundred, nearly two hundred people were sent to their deaths in Mauthausen concentration camp. Although I don't know why my life was spared, I was among the other half allowed to return home that day.

"Following that incident, my family increasingly spoke of ways to escape the predicament we now faced, but there were few possibilities. We'd thought of running away but there was nowhere to go. To leave Holland you had to cross either the Belgian, French, or Spanish border, and by then all three borders were firmly under Nazi control.

"People often ask me why we didn't go into hiding. But to do so you needed a Christian rescuer who was willing to risk his life to save yours. There were some such individuals, but of course not everyone could be hidden. Before Hitler's rise to power, there were about a hundred forty thousand Jews in Holland; after the war only thirty thousand remained. Yet of these thirty thousand, fifteen thousand, or one-half, had been hidden by Righteous Gentiles. The fact that so many of us were saved is a credit to their humanity. Sadly, many of them paid with their lives for helping our people.

"What little freedom we had left ended when the Germans came for my family. As was generally true for Dutch Jews, we were taken to the transit camp Westerbork. There were no gas chambers at Westerbork. Jews were continually transported from Westerbork to extermination centers, but we believed what we'd been told—that they were merely being transferred to other labor camps where additional help was needed.

"When my parents were sent off to be gassed, I never dreamed they'd be dead within a short time of their departure. I gave my good shoes to my father because I thought he'd need them if he did physical labor. When I saw my mother for the last time, I hugged her and told her that I hoped she wouldn't have to work too hard.

"However, not everyone was immediately gassed. I was sent to the concentration camp Bergen-Belsen. There I spent five weeks on an outdoor work detail chopping down forest trees from six o'clock in the morning until dark. We couldn't stop to rest for even a moment as we were surrounded by armed guards and German shepherd dogs that were trained to kill. Those trees weren't being cut for any particular use. If I'd remained on that detail for another week, I don't think I'd have survived.

"My next Bergen-Belsen assignment wasn't as physi-

Bergen-Belsen

cally taxing. Now I worked dismantling shoes. We initially thought we were working on old shoes which had been discarded by people in Germany but I later learned that those thousands of shoes actually belonged to gassed Jews.

"I also worked in Bergen-Belsen's kitchen, which was probably the best job available, since you were around food. Nevertheless, the hours were long—I worked from three o'clock in the morning until eight o'clock at night. But working in the kitchen didn't always mean you were well fed. I lost a close friend I'd worked with when a guard caught him smuggling out a small crust of bread. He was shot before he ever tasted it.

"Gnawing hunger was a constant problem at Bergen-Belsen. Another of my friends, who hadn't worked in the kitchen, died of starvation. So did many others at the camp, including one of my sisters. So even though Bergen-Belsen was technically not a death camp, we were frequently surrounded by death.

"At times I became despondent, but the thought of Ina kept me going. Ina was the girl I was in love with. She was at the camp as well. I kept thinking about the wonderful future we'd have together if we just survived this.

"I was later taken from Bergen-Belsen and put in a cattle car crammed with people for a fourteen-day train ride. It was actually a transport to nowhere. Although we didn't know it, those were the last days of the war. When we were finally let off the train, it was apparent that many people had died en route. I was among those made to pull the corpses from the train and place them in a mass grave we dug for them. What made it especially difficult was that some of my best friends had died. As might be expected, we were not supplied with protective clothing while completing this gruesome task. As a result of handling so many diseased bodies, I came down with spotted typhus. And at the point at which I nearly died from the illness, we were finally liberated by the Russian army.

"I was still too sick to appreciate my new freedom. I remained in a coma for five full days, but eventually pulled through. When I emerged from the coma, I only weighed seventy pounds and was extremely weak. But in time I regained my health and returned to Holland. I later married the wonderful young girl whose love had so often underscored my commitment to survive.

"Then we were two young people who'd survived the Holocaust, but today we are grandparents living in America and enjoying all the wonderful things this country has to offer. Yet we can never forget how the Holocaust cost us so many family members. My mother had seven sisters and brothers, but only four survived. My father came from a family of five children, all of whom died.

"Now when I speak about the Holocaust in public schools, students often ask me if a Holocaust survivor can ever forgive the Germans for what occurred. Forgiveness is impossible, but over the years my feelings toward the Germans have mellowed. I can't blame the younger generations of Germans for what their parents and grandparents did. I have to give them a fair chance.

"Even during the Holocaust, there had been some moral Germans who fought what Hitler was doing and were frequently killed for their defiance. Among these were many priests, ministers, and students. I owe it to these people not to condemn the entire nation.

"As long as I am able, I will continue speaking to students and other groups about the Holocaust. Six million Jews were killed—I was fortunate enough not to be. That reality obligates me to speak for those whose voices have been forever silenced. I will try to tell the world their story."

13

Ina Polak—Holland

"Perhaps we should have seen it coming, but unfortunately, we saw too few signs. The real trouble began in 1939 when Germany invaded Poland. I was sixteen years old and spending the summer in England to improve my English. I hadn't planned to return home until the end of August, but by mid-August my father called urging me to return immediately. Things were beginning to look somewhat ominous in our part of the world.

"That's only one example of how unsuspecting we were of things to come. If my father had any inkling of what lay ahead, he surely would have encouraged me to extend my stay rather than return. Of course, some Jews reasoned early on that things wouldn't go well for us and emigrated to America or Palestine [now Israel]. But at the time, their leaving was generally considered alarmist and unwarranted. My father viewed these individuals as disloyal to Holland in a way. It was incomprehensible to him that anyone could leave our beautiful country which had always treated Jews so favorably. Besides, Holland managed to stay out of World War I, and we counted on Holland

105

remaining neutral again if a second world war ever broke
out.

"I returned from England, and by May of the following year Germany invaded Belgium, France, and Holland.
In the very beginning not too much happened in Holland.
The Germans were exceedingly cunning in leading us to
believe that if we obeyed their regulations, we'd be permitted to live as we always had.

"Yet in 1942, the full-scale deportation of Holland's
Jews began. My family wasn't taken from Amsterdam to
the transit camp Westerbork until the very last transport of
Dutch Jews left in September 1943. We'd been somewhat
shielded because my father was a member of the Dutch
Jewish Council. The Germans established these councils
in each of the occupied countries to conduct their interac-
tions with the area's Jews.

"Nevertheless, our protection was not limitless. A close
friend working with the underground would often visit,
bringing us fresh vegetables to eat. This was extremely
helpful, as under the new regulations we were only permitted to shop for two hours a day. But we hadn't known
that the Nazis were aware of the woman's underground
activities and that she was being followed.

"One evening when she came to see us, the SS knocked
at our door moments later. She was immediately arrested.
Usually under these circumstances we would have been
arrested as well. Just entertaining her as our guest made us
suspect. But my father called the president of the Jewish
Council and he [the president] saw to it that we were spared.

"Yet our freedom was short-lived. One of the high-
ranking SS officers who participated in our friend's arrest
liked our living quarters. We had a luxurious spacious home
which was redecorated just prior to the war. The SS officer
was so impressed with our house that he wanted it for
himself. So the following day we were arrested anyway so
the SS officer could move in.

"We were taken to the transit camp Westerbork. We

107

were more useful to the Nazis alive than dead, as my father was one of the two leading diamond industrialists in Amsterdam, and the Germans hoped to set up a small-scale diamond plant within a concentration camp. When we were later sent from Westerbork to Bergen-Belsen [a concentration camp rather than extermination camp], everyone even remotely connected with the diamond industry was quartered in the same barracks. This included all the industry's personnel, from top diamond manufacturers to the gem cutters who shaped the stones. Although we weren't given any extra rations or privileges, we weren't made to work at the camp as other inmates were. This was to protect our hands, so we could later perform precision work on gems.

"But by the end of January 1945 when the Germans realized they were losing the war, they abandoned their plans for the Bergen-Belsen diamond factory. Nearly all the people in the diamond group were then sent to other concentration camps, where over ninety percent of them died.

"My family wasn't sent to the gas chambers because my father had somehow managed to purchase citizenship for us in El Salvador. When we were being considered for a transport, he showed the SS our official documents and impressed upon them that we couldn't be deported. He stressed that although we resided in Holland, we were still legally citizens of El Salvador, and Germany wasn't at war with El Salvador.

"But regardless of the special status we enjoyed, we knew that at any moment our situation could change. In addition, while at Bergen-Belsen, we had to contend with rampant epidemics of numerous contagious diseases, such as typhoid. I became extremely ill with several bouts of typhoid but managed to pull through.

"Near the war's end, the Germans believed that the Allies might liberate the camp within days. Therefore, we were put on a train whose destination was unknown to us.

108

There were approximately twenty-four hundred people on that train—two thousand Hungarian Jews and about four hundred Dutch Jews. All of us remained aboard for an entire week until we reached the Elbe River.

"When the train stopped at the water, we anxiously awaited what would happen next. I later learned that the conductor had been ordered by the SS to run the train off the track into the river with the Jewish passengers aboard. Luckily some of the Hungarians on the train were recently captured and still had some gold with them. They'd learned of the plot and bribed the conductor not to do it.

"Meanwhile, as we waited for something to happen, an SS officer approached the transport to reprimand the conductor for not following orders. He was furious at finding the train still safely on the track. The officer warned the conductor that the transport had better be underwater by the time he returned after lunch.

"We never saw that SS officer again, as within hours the train was liberated by American soldiers. Surprisingly, we were saved on Friday the thirteenth.

"I eventually returned to Holland, where I married Jack, the young man I'd loved all through the nightmare. We had two sons in Holland and later, when we came to America, were blessed with a daughter.

"We've had a good life here and have been happy. Still, there are images—pictures of the Holocaust that remain with me. We watched my uncle die of starvation in Bergen-Belsen and there was nothing we could do to help him. His temperature kept going down, and one morning he just didn't wake up. I'll never forget the look on his children's faces that day—they were nine and fourteen years old at the time. Their faces are part of my Holocaust memories—memories that do not become less vivid with time."

14
Solomon Fleischman—
Hungary/Transylvania

"When the war broke out I was the oldest of eleven children living with my family in Bistrita, Transylvania. We were Hasidic Jews [members of an extremely orthodox sect of Judaism.] I'd just turned sixteen when, in April 1944, we heard that all Jews were to be rounded up and taken to a ghetto outside of town.

"My father bribed a local police chief to find a hiding place for our family so that we wouldn't be taken along with the others. I remember how even at that grim moment my father still had his sense of humor. Before we left, he put two extra locks on the door to make sure the Nazis didn't have an easy time breaking into a Jewish home.

"The police chief who'd taken our money and agreed to help my family never met us as had been arranged. Perhaps he felt too much risk was involved in assisting us after all. So it looked as though we'd be left at the Nazis' mercy. My father, who'd heard stories of Polish Jews made to dig their own graves before being shot, couldn't think of a worse fate.

"Realizing that our family was too large to hide to-

111

Solomon Fleischman (back row, left) as a child with his family in Hungary. Solomon was the only family member who survived the Holocaust. Unfortunately, his mother and seven brothers and sisters were killed at Auschwitz.

gether, we had to split up. My father gathered his children around him and told us to scatter and somehow try to live through this. He'd added that if even one of us survived, his life would have been worthwhile. Then he took out all his money and divided it up among us. Even my infant sister had money tucked in her clothes in the hope that a kind Gentile might rescue her.

"My father and one of my brothers hid from the Nazis together. In the end, my mother chose to remain in our apartment with the smaller children and be taken to the ghetto along with the others in our building. However, I decided to leave and try to hide. I felt I might be of more help to my mother and siblings on the outside and might even find a way to rescue them.

"I knew of a hiding place directly beneath our building. A cellar, which ran the full length of the structure, connected with a stairway that led directly to a small, cavelike space. I brought candles, matches, blankets, bread, and some ration coupons down to my tiny dwelling to stock it as well as possible. I decided not to tell any of my family where I'd be hiding. If we didn't know each other's hiding places, then we couldn't betray one another if we were captured and tortured by the Nazis. Although the cellar had cubicles which contained tenant property, I didn't think anyone knew about the small hiding space below it.

"But when I went down to settle in, I was startled to see someone already there. To my relief it was just one of my uncles, who heard of the space through my father. He asked me if he could remain. There was barely enough room and supplies for one person, but I couldn't turn my back on him.

"On our first day in hiding, we established an important survival rule. We vowed never to speak out loud so the sound of our voices wouldn't reveal our whereabouts. On the other side of the wall was a German barber who was half deaf anyway. When he wasn't busy he'd play the violin between customers. Listening to his music was one

113

of our few pleasures. Otherwise, my uncle and I generally spent our time contending with having little to eat while living in a space too small to stretch out in.

"After a week, when we exhausted our food supply, my uncle and I weren't sure of our next move. I'd begun thinking about a fourteen-year-old Christian apprentice working in the carpentry shop above us whom I'd previously befriended. Since I knew he arrived for work at the shop about a half hour earlier than the others, my uncle and I agreed that I should approach him.

"The next morning, as the apprentice was about to enter the shop, I opened the cellar door and called out to him. As he turned to face me, his mouth dropped open in amazement. The boy immediately came into the cellar and hugged me. He agreed to help us using my ration coupons to bring us bread every three days. But one day after about three weeks, I heard someone else open the cellar door and call my name. It was the Christian carpentry shop owner— a young family man of Romanian descent with two small children. He'd said, 'Come out, I know you're here. Don't worry, I'll take care of you.'

"My uncle told me to go to him, thinking that perhaps our prayers had been answered. But I decided to remain silent until he [the shop owner] left. Still, when he returned the next day, I acknowledged our presence. He hugged and kissed me and told me how glad he was that I was alive. When I inquired how conditions were in the Jewish ghetto, he said that things had gone badly for the residents. He described how people suspected of having hidden gold or silver were savagely beaten by the Nazis. Food there was scarce, while disease was rampant.

"The carpentry shop owner had found out about my uncle and me when he had followed his apprentice after noticing the boy carrying some extra bread rations. After confronting the fourteen-year-old, the youth broke down and confessed that he'd helped us. Now the kind Christian carpenter assured us that our survival and safety no longer rested with a child. He promised that from then on, he'd take care of us.

"The Righteous Romanian Gentile who saved both my uncle and me was Valeriu Moldovan. He continued to bring us food regularly and refused to accept what little money I tried to give him in return. More than once Moldovan risked his life to protect us. Once while I'd dared to exercise in the cellar adjacent to our tiny dwelling, I was suddenly intruded on by two carpentry shop foremen. The men had broken into an empty apartment above us and stashed satchels of stolen goods in the cellar. When they'd come to retrieve the items, they'd seen me.

"The two pretended to befriend me and asked if they could help in any way. But a few days later, Mr. Moldovan described how they'd told him about me and suggested that the three of them beat me up to find out if my family had hidden any silver or gold in or near the building. They'd added that once they obtained the information they could kill me and bury my body in the cellar. Moldovan told them that if they touched me he'd report them to the authorities for the break-ins and robberies they committed on the premises. As the foremen knew they could receive the death penalty for their actions, the matter was dropped.

"There were also other near disasters. The government reopened our apartment house for Gentiles, and Mr. Moldovan told me that two Secret Service detectives moved into one of the upstairs apartments. He'd described both men in detail to me for my own protection, but I hoped I'd never have cause to see either. Then one day I took a senseless risk. It was a beautiful Indian summer September morning, and after having been cooped up for months, I felt I just had to step out of the cellar for a moment to feel the sun and breathe the air.

"But as I opened the cellar door, I'd found myself face-to-face with one of the detectives. I instantly retreated, closing the cellar door from inside. Meanwhile, the detective had begun to bang on the door as he yelled

115

Valeriu Moldovan, the Romanian gentleman who saved the lives of Mr. Fleischman and his uncle

for me to let him in. Then a few moments later he left. While he was gone I removed the door's hinge, so it would instantly open if the detective returned to try it again. I wanted him to think I'd run off leaving the door open. As I waited to see what would happen next, I hid some distance away in the cellar's darkness.

"As I suspected, the detective soon returned with a key to the cellar door. But when he turned the key in the lock, the door gave way, causing him to fall into the cellar. He was hurt slightly and began cursing and screaming, 'Where are you? Come out right now.'

"A Christian woman living upstairs who was a close friend of my mother's heard all the commotion and came downstairs to ask the detective what was going on. He told her that he saw a boy in the cellar who just seemed to have vanished. The woman, who knew I was hiding somewhere, thought I might be the boy seen by the detective and quickly concocted a story to save me. She said, 'Oh, that must have been the carpenter's apprentice. He's an orphan and usually comes here on Sundays to wash himself and clean his clothes.' Satisfied with her explanation, the detective left and never came back.

"By October 1944, Russian forces had begun to bombard the city. As fearful civilians left the area in droves, our city seemed to rapidly turn into a ghost town. Mr. Moldovan came by to leave us an ample supply of bread and say good-bye. Soon afterwards, when my uncle and I heard Russian soldiers' voices coming from the street, we felt it was safe to leave our underground hiding place. By then we'd lived in the tiny enclosure for over five months and were barely able to walk when we first stood up. But the sunlight still felt warm and wonderful on our faces. The Russians gave us food, and Jewish Russian soldiers held services in our local synagogue.

"I was alive and liberated, but I later learned that I was the only member of my immediate family to survive. My father and brother's hiding place was revealed to the

Nazis by an informer. They'd hidden in the woods with some friends who brought along an infant. When the baby became ill, the child's father tried to find some aspirin and came across a Gentile farmer who agreed to help. But the following day, the Nazis came to the forest with dogs and arrested all of them. For betraying them, the farmer-informer received the price of a cow. On a broader scale, the human annihilation had been comparably massive. Only a hundred and twenty-five of the ten thousand Jews who lived in my city survived."

Author's note: Solomon Fleischman settled in America after living in Israel for a time. Following the war, he sent Mr. Moldovan money and gifts. After Moldovan died, Mr. Fleischman continued sending items to both his son and grandson. He also ships coffee, tea, chocolate, and other articles to the quick-thinking woman who dissuaded the detective from searching for him. Today, Solomon Fleischman has five children and seventeen grandchildren, none of whom would be with us had it not been for those who jeopardized their own lives to save his.

15

Helen Kornitzer Laitman —Czechoslovakia/Hungary

"I was one of three sisters born into an orthodox Jewish family in Czechoslovakia. My parents were strict but loving, and I enjoyed a happy childhood.

"In Czechoslovakia Jews had been an accepted part of the general population. But in the years to come, sweeping anti-Semitism and the Nazi invasion changed all that. By 1942 the Nazis began deporting Jews. Boys were taken into forced labor, while some young girls were shipped off to brothels to be prostitutes for German soldiers. My father was determined to find a way for my younger sister and me to leave the country. He used whatever funds were available to him to buy us a means by which to travel to Hungary. Hungary may not have been an ideal getaway, but by then borders throughout Europe were closed to Jews, and at the time German troops weren't yet present in Hungary.

"My eleven-year-old sister and I fled through the woods until we reached a town near the Hungarian border. My father arranged for Gypsies familiar with the area's terrain to help us board a nearby train for Hungary. Although we

had false papers, it would have been disastrous if we were stopped and questioned. My sister and I both spoke Hungarian so poorly that we couldn't have convinced anyone that we'd been born and raised there.

"When we arrived in Budapest, we headed directly for my aunt's home. We couldn't live there openly since we were illegal aliens and technically should not have even been in the country. At first, we tried never to show our faces unless it was absolutely necessary. If we left the building at all, we'd take the back stairs rather than the elevator. But it was safest for us to remain on the move. Whenever we stayed with anyone, we always said we were their visiting nieces from the countryside. Having to pack up and move every few months was unsettling, but necessary. At least during this time my little sister attended what appeared to be a Catholic school but was actually a school for Jewish children.

"As I was older, I decided to use my Aryan features and fair hair to help other Jews hiding illegally in Hungary or being oppressed by the Nazi regime in other countries. I began working as a courier for the underground. I'd successfully exchanged my false Hungarian documents for Polish papers. As I spoke Polish fluently, the chances of my being detected by the authorities greatly lessened.

"Before long we watched German troops march into Hungary. Although I'd told my Hungarian Jewish friends how the Nazis dealt with Jews just across the border in Czechoslovakia, they hadn't believed me until they encountered it themselves. Prior to tackling the large cities, the Nazis began deporting Hungarian Jews from the outlying towns and hamlets. However, they'd met some resistance from a group of Jewish men and boys who refused to be quietly led to the slaughter. These Jewish males gathered together near the Romanian border to prepare to fight.

"The underground was anxious to help this faction in their struggle. On three separate occasions, I was sent to

121

Helen Laitman as a young woman. Her fair hair and features helped her survive the Holocaust.

bring them both money and guns. I was also instrumental in supplying valuable intelligence information to them. I believe their eventual goal was to join up with the Russian army to fight the Nazis.

"Each time I traveled by train to meet with them. To appear as relaxed and natural as possible, I'd try to ingratiate myself with the other passengers. On one trip, our train stopped across from the cattle car filled with Jews. The pain and anguish evident on those individuals' faces were appalling. Yet apparently the sight hadn't stirred pity in those around me. One passenger commented on how good it was to finally be rid of the Jews, while some others seemed to be in agreement. It was difficult to hear them speak that way, knowing that I could have just as easily been on that cattle car as aboard the comfortable train I rode.

"Within a short time, the Nazis turned their attention from persecuting Jews in the countryside to those in the cities. Budapest Jews were soon crowded into a ghetto. Wherever you looked, Jews were being randomly killed. A limited number of Hungarian Jews were saved by flocking inside the embassies of Sweden and Switzerland. These were "safe house" of sorts, and those who made it inside couldn't be touched by the Nazis. Working with the underground, I had a pass to come and go from such locations, and was therefore able to bring food and messages to those inside. When the situation was at its worst, I luckily found a place for my aunt in the Swedish embassy, and she survived the war."

Author's note: Helen Laitman and her younger sister survived the Holocaust, but there were some close calls. Once when she'd tried to leave the country, Laitman was caught by the SS while crossing the border. As she waited in a cell, she'd heard the screams of others being interrogated and beaten. One of the SS officers refused to believe she

123

was a Christian Pole and insisted she was Jewish. Convinced he could make her talk, he had her receive twenty-five lashes. However, despite the brutality, Helen Laitman clung to her story and her silence saved her life. With the underground's assistance, she was eventually freed.

16
Clara Knopfler—
Transylvania

"I was just thirteen years old when German-occupied Hungary took over Transylvania where my family lived. Although I hadn't known it then, my life would be changed forever by the events to come. Before long, anti-Jewish laws were enacted. My father, who formerly manufactured and sold shoes, was forbidden to continue his business. We couldn't go out to movies, parks, and many other public places where we'd be harassed and humiliated.

"As our Christian friends saw what was happening, they began to distance themselves from us. I think they feared possible repercussions from associating with Jews. We felt isolated and alone as we continued to be concerned about what might happen next.

"On May 3, 1944, we were taken from our home by soldiers. There was no time to pack your favorite things, as you were only given a few minutes to gather some flour and a few edible items. All books, furniture, jewelry, and other valuables had to be left behind. The soldiers then transported us to a fenced-off Jewish ghetto. Ten thousand people brought together from different regions were made

125

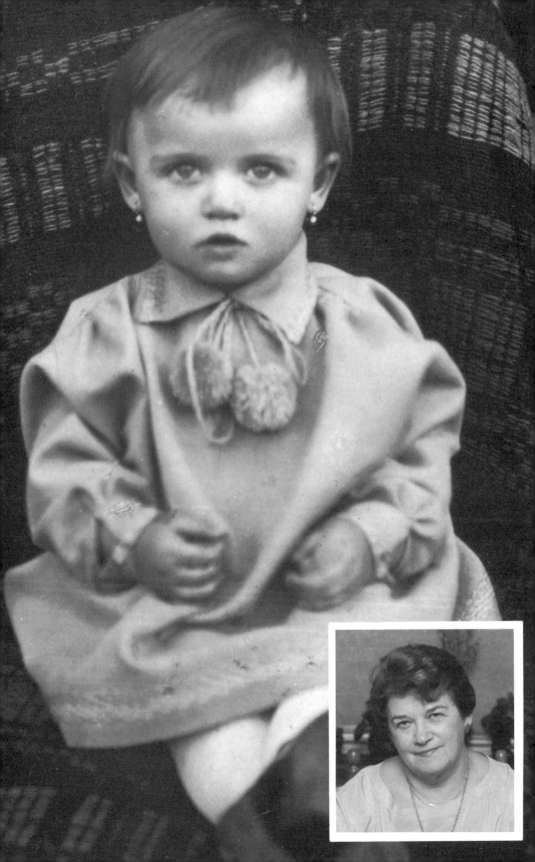

to reside in a large brick factory building. Twenty to twenty-five people were crowded into one room. Since there were no walls or panel dividers, we put up sheets to afford individual families some degree of privacy.

"Ghetto living conditions were deplorable. There were no toilet facilities for the ten thousand residents. We were forced to urinate and defecate in large outdoor trenches. The guards did not permit any privacy as they'd been instructed to carefully observe us. Some guards suspected us of having swallowed diamonds prior to our leaving our homes, which they thought we might later retrieve from our feces.

"Our guards took turns brutalizing ghetto residents. My father, along with a number of other men, was severely beaten. They wanted the men to confess if they'd hidden any valuables in or around their homes prior to leaving. Apparently, some people suspected that our belongings would be confiscated, so they buried gold items and jewelry in their yards hoping to come back for the booty when the war was over.

"After a few weeks of living in the ghetto, we were deported to Auschwitz, an extermination camp in eastern Poland. Prior to our departure, my uncle contemplated taking his own life as well as the lives of his wife and two young children. But we managed to dissuade him, never imagining that the four would soon be killed anyway.

"We traveled to Auschwitz in a cattle car tightly packed with at least seventy people. During the four- to five-day trip to the camp, we were unable to lie down due to the lack of space. We slept standing up pressed against one another. The Nazis had not provided toilet facilities for their human cargo. At least two people in my car died along the way.

"We arrived at Auschwitz at eleven o'clock at night. Immediately after stepping off the train, the men and women were separated as were the old from the young. My mother and I quickly lost track of my father and brother, but we

127

later learned that both of them died. My brother, a promising young pianist, refused to do road work and stone cutting for the Nazis, knowing it would destroy his hands for his career. So the Nazis shot him.

"Although my mother was forty-two at the time, she actually looked much younger. Therefore she was placed with a group of fairly young women. She thought it strange that she wasn't with the other women her age, but as none of the other mothers were with us, I just felt glad to have her near me. Neither of us realized that my mother's youthful appearance saved her life that night. The older women were immediately gassed, while the younger ones had been spared for the moment. As long as we remained healthy, we would serve as a slave labor force for the Nazis.

"Of course, youth wasn't always an advantage. At seventeen, I was among the youngest Jews from the transport who were not gassed. Children under sixteen or seventeen years of age weren't considered strong enough to be useful and were often systematically killed.

"After the Nazis completed their gassing selections, the women in my group were taken for a shower and haircut. We were all given crew cuts. Their humiliation of us was immediate. We stood naked in front of SS officers who paced back and forth looking us over to determine which girls would be used as prostitutes for the German soldiers who fought in various parts of the world. However, all women remaining in the camps were treated solely as prisoners. An SS member caught having sex with a Jew might be severely punished or even executed.

"Some survived Auschwitz, but no one escaped the tremendous abuse characteristic of the camp's treatment of its prisoners. While at Auschwitz, we had to endure roll calls as often as five times daily. These might be held at any hour of the day or night. Frequently, we stood outside in the pouring rain for four or five hours while SS officers determined who'd live and who would die.

"My mother and I were only at Auschwitz for about

five days before being sent to the work camp Kaiserwald in Latvia. There I worked in a gunpowder factory. We labored from six in the evening until six in the morning and were hardly given any food. Often exhausted women fell asleep while working. Then, without warning, a guard would beat them. One of the guards was a bit more compassionate than the others. He asked who among us was able to sing. When I told him I could, he told me to sing as loudly as possible because if I didn't keep the women awake and working he'd be forced to beat them.

"Handling gunpowder was messy work, so we were usually covered with dirt and grime when we left the factory each morning. Then we'd be sent to shower, but as the showers were some distance away, to get there we had to walk on a camp road made of tombstones from a Jewish cemetery desecrated by the Nazis. As the soles of our shoes touched the engraved tombstone letters of the names of those deceased, I remember thinking what an abomination this was. It was still hard to believe this was really happening to human beings.

"We showered with cold water, and since we had no soap it was difficult to become really clean. After a few weeks, the guards realized that we were unable to function this way so they gave us soap. But when we saw what the soap was made of, we couldn't use it. It had been manufactured from the remains of Jewish bodies and bore a stamp which read, MADE FROM PURE JEWISH FAT. I had no way of knowing if the fat used in the soap was my father's, my brother's, or whose.

"We later learned that when Jews were gassed at some extermination camps such as Auschwitz, their bodies weren't always taken directly to the crematorium to be burned. Too many corpses were frequently produced to fuel the ovens simultaneously. Depending on the circumstances, one to three hundred people might die at once. Their freshly gassed bodies would be laid outside on the ground and used as raw materials for German products. Their hair was stuffed into pillows and mattresses, their fat used to make soap, and their bones sent to German glue factories. The gold from their tooth fillings was extracted and used to help support the Nazi cause.

"When we first arrived at Kaiserwald, we still had no idea that a massive execution of Jews was already well under way. We'd seen the crematoriums at Auschwitz but thought they were for people who'd died of disease and starvation. Who would have dreamed that gas chambers especially designed to kill large numbers of human beings had been created?

"We witnessed selections, but we hadn't realized that those individuals were selected to die. We thought that perhaps they were being sent to the infirmary or assigned less exhausting duties. But after a while we began to see that Jews were dying in large numbers, even though we still weren't aware of gas chambers. I'd realized they'd built a new extermination center near Kaiserwald after my cousin happened to be sent to our camp. It was wonderful to see her again. I'd only remained with my mother, and we'd wondered about other family members often. Now the three of us cried and hugged one another.

"But after two or three days, we heard that my cousin and the others she arrived with were being taken away. We didn't know where they were going, but by four o'clock that afternoon we found out when their dresses and other clothing were brought back to our camp. The only conclusion we could come to was that these young girls had been killed.

"As the months passed, the war wound down. The Germans knew they were losing and wanted to quickly rid themselves of both the killing centers and inmates who might eventually testify against them. So the selections at our camp increased and more and more people continued to disappear.

"Whether or not you were chosen to die often had a great deal to do with your appearance. Those of us who looked strong might be allowed to live a while longer. They'd check your legs to see if your limbs were still muscular and firm. You also had a better chance of remaining alive if you hadn't grown too thin or pale. A Jewish young man who came to the camp tried to help both my mother and me. He was an expert at repairing industrial machinery. This skill kept him alive during the war, since the Nazis took full advantage of his talents. Whenever the machinery at our gunpowder factory broke down, he was called to fix it.

"The last time I saw him he warned me that a massive selection would be held at Kaiserwald in two days. He gave me a piece of red paper and told me to rub its dye off on my mother's cheeks to make her look young and in good health. He also gave me a scarf to wear around my head to improve my appearance.

"On the day of the selection, as we were inspected by the SS, I heard an officer ask my mother her age. I knew they planned to kill the older individuals first. My mother was in her early forties, but she lied about her age and said that she was thirty-nine. The SS officer glared at her angrily and said, 'How dare you lie to me? Are you anxious to die? You're not fooling me; I can see that you're not even thirty-five yet.' I breathed a sigh of relief as I watched him walk on to the next person. My mother had been spared.

"The SS felt they couldn't keep the camp operating any longer as they knew that Russian soldiers were already swarming the region. Kaiserwald was evacuated. The four thousand inmates were put on a merchandise ship which sailed to Danzig, Poland. The conditions on board were horrid. Six women had to share one bed and we were only given bread and lard to eat, which made us both thirsty and ill. Many died during the passage. When we arrived at Danzig, we saw at least two hundred corpses tossed into the sea.

"From there we were taken to a camp called Stuthof,

131

where a further selection was made. Apparently, my mother and I were still considered healthy enough to work, so instead of being killed we were sent to another work camp in east Germany near the villages of Guttau and Dörbeck. There we had to dig antitank trenches to incapacitate Russian artillery. These ditches were both six yards wide and deep. We shoveled dirt every day from five o'clock in the morning until seven at night. It was hard physical labor, and if you didn't dig fast enough, you were beaten.

"We were housed in tents which did little to keep out the cold as winter approached, and we had only a thin blanket for warmth at night. During the day, my mother and I continued to wear the threadbare cotton dresses we'd been issued months before at Auschwitz. Disease spread through the camp, as many inmates came down with typhoid fever. If you became ill, you were allowed to stop work for half a day. Then if you still weren't well enough to work you were shot. Many young women died due to contagious diseases, our punishing work regime, and poor sanitary conditions. Nearly every morning you'd wake up to find another corpse in your tent. But before they died, many of these girls begged the rest of us to fight to stay alive so we could tell the world what happened to them.

"As it was near the end of the war and German manpower was dwindling, our guards were assisted by young people from Hitler's Youth who supervised the prisoners at work. Some of these young boys were trained to be quite brutal. Once one of them began to beat my mother for not working fast enough. I couldn't stand to watch him— this was the only time I openly rebelled as I felt I had little left to lose. I yelled out at the boy, 'Don't hit my mother. She's working as hard as she can. She's starving, she's not allowed to rest, and she still keeps working. Don't you have a mother, can't you feel for her?' I knew I could be killed for speaking out that way, but I felt I had to do it.

"The boy stopped hitting my mother and didn't come after me. He only answered, 'Yes, I have a mother, but

132

she's not a Jew.' Yet I must have touched something inside him because the next day he brought me a carrot and half a cigarette. I didn't smoke, but he told me that smoking it would help to dull my hunger pangs.

"Soon the Christmas season came. On Christmas Eve I, along with several other girls, decided to sneak out of the camp for an hour. We hoped that while in the holiday spirit the local people would give their food scraps to some starving girls. We managed to leave and return undetected, and before long we were back dividing up the food with my mother and the others. But two of the girls were spotted giving out some bread. An SS officer took them to the center of the camp, where he poured ice water over them. They were made to stay out in the freezing cold all night wearing only their soaking-wet cotton dresses. By morning both had frozen to death. This was how the Christian SS officer spent Christmas.

"By January 19, Russian troops were so close we could hear their gunfire. Only about two hundred and fifty of the one thousand women we originally worked with were still alive. The SS did not want the Russians to find either them or us, so we were taken on a death march. We called it a death march because if someone was unable to walk or keep up with the others, she was shot and left along the roadside.

"We continued like this for two days until we came to a German farm. The SS officers rested and had a meal. Some of the inmates overheard them discussing what to do with us. One suggested shooting us, but the others argued that would waste bullets they might later need to defend themselves against the Russians. Another favored burning us alive, but they decided that would leave too much of a mess for their hospitable farm family. To our good fortune, they settled the matter by running away to save themselves and abandoning us where we were.

"Then my mother and I began the long ten-week trip back to our home. We begged for food and rides along the

133

way and usually spent our nights sleeping in empty school-houses. When we finally arrived, I learned that a Gentile girlfriend had hidden my accordion and my favorite navy blue velvet dress for me. After what we'd been through, I had nothing. I was dirty, there were lice in my hair, and I had no underwear. But I owned an accordion and that party dress.

"My immediate family originally consisted of my father, mother, brother, and myself. My mother came from a family of five and my father from a family of eleven. Four members of my father's family came to the United States prior to World War II, and they were saved from the Nazi ravages. However, of the others, only my mother, one cousin, and I survived. We lost a total of thirty-four family members through the Holocaust.

"Today I feel I have to talk about the Holocaust to let people know how so many innocent lives were taken. Often during speaking engagements, I am asked how I was able to regain my faith in others following my ordeal. I can only say that many of my positive feelings grew out of the friendship and acceptance I experienced when I returned home from the camps. I believe there is kindness and decency in everyone. It's a matter of touching each person's humanity and building on it to create a better world for us all."

Glossary

Crystal Night (the Night of Broken Glass)—on November 9, 1938, the glass windows of Jewish stores and homes were shattered, synagogues were set on fire, and many Jews were terrorized, beaten, and deported to concentration camps; that night was an ominous sign of the Nazis' forthcoming systematic persecution of Jews

deportation—the process by which Jews and other minorities were expelled from their homes and/or countries and forcibly taken to various Nazi camps

Gentile—any person who is not of the Jewish faith; the term usually refers to Christian individuals

Gestapo—Hitler's dreaded secret police known for their brutal tactics; while the Gestapo began as a separate unit in 1933, it was integrated into Germany's standard police force by 1936

Hitler Youth, or Hitler's Youth—a compulsory youth organization for German boys and girls designed to ensure allegiance to Hitler; activities generally included marching and exercising as well as a firm indoctrination to Nazi beliefs *partisans*—patriotic civilians who banded together to fight German rule and oppression within their country; for example, partisans sabotaged munitions trains and committed other destructive acts to hinder the Nazi presence

Righteous Gentiles—non-Jews who helped save Jewish lives

SS (Schutzstaffel)—Hitler's elitist private Aryan army of guards; those in the prestigious SS were skilled in sophisticated military tactics, as opposed to the street-fighting style and demeanor characteristic of Hitler's storm troopers (see below)

storm troopers—uniformed men who served as armed thugs for the Nazi Party

transit camp—a camp or other area where Jews were assembled before being transported to concentration camps or extermination centers

underground—a secret organization of civilians, sometimes aided by military personnel, actively engaged in harassing, destroying, and generally creating havoc among the Nazis

Holocaust Organizations

Auschwitz Study Foundation, Inc.
P.O. Box 2232
Huntington Beach, California 92647

Bund Archives of the Jewish
	Labor Movement
26 East 21st Street, 3rd floor
New York, New York 10003

Center for Holocaust and
	Genocide Studies
Ramapo College Library
505 Ramapo Valley Road
Mahwah, New Jersey 07430

Center for Holocaust Studies
Brookdale Community College
765 Newman Springs Road
Lincroft, New Jersey 07738

Center for Holocaust Studies
Documentation and Research
1610 Avenue J
Brooklyn, New York 11230

Commission on Holocaust
	Remembrance of
	Agudath Israel
	of America
84 William Street
New York, New York 10038

Fred R. Crawford Witness to
	the Holocaust Project
Emory University
Atlanta, Georgia 30067

The Dallas Memorial Center
	for Holocaust Studies
7900 Northaven Road
Dallas, Texas 75230

El Paso Holocaust Museum
	and Study Center
405 Wallenberg Drive
El Paso, Texas 79912

Facing History and Ourselves,
  National Foundation Inc.
25 Kennard Road
Brookline, Massachusetts 02146

Fortunoff Video Archive for
  Holocaust Testimonies
Sterling Memorial Library
Room 331-C
Yale University
New Haven, Connecticut 06520

Friends of Le Chambon
8033 Sunset Boulevard
No. 784
Los Angeles, California 90046

Greater Cincinnati Interfaith
  Holocaust Foundation
3101 Clifton Avenue
Cincinnati, Ohio 45220

Holocaust Archive
Gratz College
Melrose Park, Pennsylvania 19126

Holocaust Awareness Institute
University of Denver
Denver, Colorado 80208

Holocaust Center of the Jewish
  Federation of the
  North Shore
McCarthy School, Room 108
70 Lake Street
Peabody, Massachusetts 01960

The Holocaust Center
  of Minneapolis
8200 West 33rd Street
Minneapolis, Minnesota 55426

The Holocaust Center of Northern
  California
639 14th Street
San Francisco, California 94118

Holocaust Center for the
  United Jewish Federation
  of Greater Pittsburgh
242 McKee Place
Pittsburgh, Pennsylvania 15213

Holocaust Documentation
  Education Center, Inc.
Florida International University
North Miami Campus
N.E. 151 Street & Biscayne Blvd.
North Miami, Florida 33181

Holocaust Education and
  Documentation Centre
4600 Bathurst Street
Willowdale, Ontario
Canada M2R 3V2

Holocaust Human Rights
  Center of Maine
Box 825
Palermo, Maine 04354

Holocaust Learning Center
5850 South Pine Island Road
Davie, Florida 33328

Holocaust Memorial
  Foundation of Illinois
4255 West Main Street
Skokie, Illinois 60076

Holocaust Memorial
  Resource & Education
  Center of Central
  Florida
851 N. Maitland Avenue
Maitland, Florida 32751

Holocaust Resource Center
Keene State College
229 Main Street
Keene, New Hampshire 03431

138

Holocaust Resource Center
Bureau of Jewish Education
441 East Avenue
Rochester, New York 14607

Holocaust Resource
Center and Archives
Queensborough Community College
56th Avenue & Springfield Blvd.
Bayside, New York 11364

Holocaust Resource
Center of Buffalo
2640 North Forest Road
Getzville, New York 14068

Holocaust Resource Center
of Greater Toledo
6465 Sylvania Avenue
Sylvania, Ohio 43560

Holocaust Survivors
and Friends in Pursuit
of Justice, Inc.
800 New Loudon Road
Suite No. 400
Latham, New York 12110

Interfaith Council on
the Holocaust
125 South 9th Street
Philadelphia, Pennsylvania 19107

International Network
of Children of
Jewish Holocaust
Survivors, Inc.
Florida International University
North Miami Campus—SC 130
N.E. 151st Street & Biscayne Blvd.
North Miami, Florida 33181

Long Island Center
for Holocaust Studies
261 Willis Avenue
Mineola, New York 11501

Martyrs Memorial and Museum
of the Jewish
Federation Council
6505 Wilshire Blvd.
Los Angeles, California 90048

Joseph Meyerhoff Library
Baltimore Hebrew University
5800 Park Heights Avenue
Baltimore, Maryland 21215

The Montreal Holocaust
Memorial Centre
5151 Cote
Ste. Catherine Road
Montreal, Quebec
Canada H3W 1M6

National Association for
Holocaust Education
West Chester University
West Chester, Pennsylvania 19383

Oregon Holocaust
Resource Center
2900 SW Peaceful Lane
Portland, Oregon 97201

Rhode Island Holocaust
Memorial Museum
JCC of Rhode Island
401 Elmgrove Avenue
Providence, Rhode Island 02906

Rockland Center for
Holocaust Studies, Inc.
17 South Madison Avenue
Spring Valley, New York 10977

St. Louis Center for
Holocaust Studies
12 Millstone Campus Drive
St. Louis, Missouri 63146

Simon Wiesenthal Center
9760 West Pico Boulevard
Los Angeles, California 90035

139

For Further Reading

BOOKS

Adler, David. *We Remember the Holocaust*. New York: Holt, 1989.

Frank, Anne. *The Works of Anne Frank*. Westport, Conn.: Greenwood, 1974.

Friedman, Ina R. *The Other Victims: First-Person Stories of Non-Jews Persecuted by the Nazis*. Boston: Houghton Mifflin, 1990.

Landau, Elaine. *Nazi War Criminals*. New York: Franklin Watts, 1990.

Meltzer, Milton. *Never to Forget: The Jews of the Holocaust*. New York: Harper & Row, 1976.

Ramati, Alexander. *And the Violins Stopped Playing: A Story of the Gypsy Holocaust*. New York: Franklin Watts, 1986.

Rossel, Seymour. *The Holocaust*. New York: Franklin Watts, 1981.

Roth-Hano, Renee. *Touch Wood: A Girlhood in Occupied France*. New York: Penguin, 1989.

Sender, Ruth Minsky. *The Cage*. New York: Macmillan, 1986.

Storm, Yale. *A Tree Still Stands: Jewish Youth in Eastern Europe Today*. New York: Philomel/Putnam, 1990.

ARTICLES

"Hitler's Grab For World Power," by John Keegan. *U.S. News & World Report,* vol. 107, August 28, 1989, p. 34.

"The Holocaust: Why the Jews?" by Tamar Jacoby. *Newsweek,* vol. 113, May 15, 1989, p. 64.

"Holocaust Museum: A Troubled Start," by Judith Miller. *New York Times Magazine,* April 22, 1990, p. 34.

"An Interview With Elie Wiesel," by Carol Rittner. *America,* vol. 159, November 19, 1988, p. 397.

"Killing Field" (filming of *Triumph of the Spirit*), by Antonin Kratochvil. *Premiere,* vol. 3, December 1989, p. 118.

"Legacy of Kristallnacht Stirs Different Emotions: After 50 Years, Some Jews Find Hope, Others Despair," by Ann Johnson. *National Catholic Reporter,* vol. 25, November 25, 1988, p. 30.

"Music Box: Joe Eszterhas Writes a Wrong" (screenwriter explains why he wrote this film about the Holocaust in Hungary), by Robert Seidenberg. *American Film,* vol. 15, February 1990, p. 51.

"A Nation Haunted Still" (German history and politics), by Henrik Bering-Jensen. *Insight,* vol. 5, March 20, 1989, p. 13.

"A Nation Overshadowed" (Austria). *The Economist,* vol. 306, March 12, 1988, p. 83.

"The Night That Shattered Humanity" (anniversary of Kristallnacht, or Crystal Night, anti-Jewish rampage in Third Reich). *U.S. News & World Report,* vol. 105, November 14, 1988, p. 14.

"Not All the Wounds Have Healed" (Terezin, Czechoslovakia), by Richard Z. Chesnoff. *U.S. News & World Report,* vol. 108, March 5, 1990, p. 36.

"The Past Underfoot" (German Holocaust memorials). *The Economist,* vol. 310, February 4, 1989, p. 88.

"Perversions of the Holocaust" (analysis of current interpretations), by Lucy S. Davidowicz. *Commentary,* vol. 88, October 1989, p. 56.

"Remembrance and Responsibility" (courage to face the truth of the Holocaust), by Guenthar Roth. *Society,* vol. 26, March-April 1989, p. 4.

"Unlocking History" (Western scholars allowed access to Nazi and Soviet documents on Holocaust). *U.S. News & World Report,* vol. 105, August 29, 1988, p. 14.

"Visiting the Burnt House" (Auschwitz), by Hana Bloch. *Tikkun,* vol. 4, May-June 1989, p. 45.

Index

Page numbers in *italics* indicate illustrations.